Fishing Dogs

Fishing Dogs

A Guide to the History, Talents, and
Training of the Baildale,
the Flounderhounder,
the Angler Dog, and Sundry Other
Breeds of Aquatic Dogs
(Canis piscatorius)

Raymond Coppinger
Illustrated by Peter Pinardi
Foreword by Nick Lyons

Skyhorse Publishing

Skyhorse Publishing books may be purchased in bulk at special discounts for sales promotion, corporate gifts, fund-raising, or educational purposes. Special editions can also be created to specifications. For details, contact the Special Sales Department, Skyhorse Publishing, 307 West 36th Street, 11th Floor, New York, NY 10018 or info@skyhorsepublishing.com.

Skyhorse® and Skyhorse Publishing® are registered trademarks of Skyhorse Publishing, Inc.®, a Delaware corporation.

www.skyhorsepublishing.com

10 9 8 7 6 5 4 3 2 1

Library of Congress Cataloging-in-Publication Data is available on file.

ISBN: 978-1-62636-555-1

Printed in China

Since I still can't think of anyone better,
I again dedicate this book to Stan Warner.

Contents

Acknowledgments

Old Giller (1928–1940)

Rumor has it that Barnaby Porter, the discoverer of the bow-plunk breed of dog, has converted a historic old building in Damariscotta, Maine, into the Fishing Dog Hall of Fame. There he teaches evening writing courses and has sent two prize-winning essays, written by Craig Kling and Ken McCort, to be included herein. My warmest thanks to all three of you.

There are literally hundreds of people involved in writing a book to greater or lesser extent—mostly the latter. In the "greater extent" category is Rae-Ann Wentworth, computer specialist at Hampshire College, who figured out where the manuscript had gone (after some technical difficulties), and several people on her staff, who prepared and delivered lectures to me about backing up documents. Equally warm thanks to her and them.

Winner of the "lesser extent" category is Dr. Ramon Escobedo-Martinez of the Department of Intelligent Design Cosinus Magnus of the Basque Center for Mathematical Dog Research. His suggestion was about grappling (means: dragging your hook along the bottom) with the angle of refraction of the real imaginary line of looking by pike pointers. Creatively, he did the calculations in old Basque Mathematical notation (Roman Numerals). Unfortunately, the publisher has a rule about publishing in foreign languages so those calculations will appear elsewhere. I would like to thank him here so his name doesn't have to appear elsewhere.

The original drawings for this book by Peter Pinardi were shredded into strips by a white-footed deer mouse (*Peromyscus leocopus*). She used those strips to build a gigantic artistic labyrinth where she raised four lovely offspring (three girls and a boy). After the mouse finished her reproductive activities, Dave Pinardi (Peter's brother) of Adagio Graphic Designs and his helpers carefully reassembled all of them. Lorna Coppinger, working behind the scenes, was able to make them look somewhat like the originals in just a few short months. (We decided not to do the book in color because of some yellow staining, which I personally thought made the drawings more interesting.) Warmest thanks to you all.

Unlike those mentioned above, there were several people who actually had a good time helping with the various aspects of writing of the book. The pleasure they got will suffice and there is no need to mention them, but you know who you are. More warm thanks.

Thanks to you all,

Ray Coppinger

Foreword

What a lot of fun you'll have reading *Fishing Dogs*—a dry, wry, witty, persistently cunning exploration of "how to train fishing dogs," "new uses for fishing dogs," "how to make a fishing dog," and much more you've never thought of before. In fact, if you didn't read the author's previous book—which too few folk did—you may not even have imagined there *were* "fishing dogs," whatever they are, but when you read this book, you'll surely know.

Here you'll learn it all, from their first discovery to their evolution, and special breeds that came about—gillie dogs, bilge pups, baildales, fish-spotter dogs, dogfishing dogs . . . Ray even tells you how to make your own dog. You've probably read plenty about hunting dogs, and seen all of the art, photographs, and books about them. But fishing dogs have been sadly neglected. One of the purposes of this book is to put the many new discoveries about these breeds "in phylogenetic order and bring you up to date" on what the author calls "The Wonderful World of Fishing Dogs."

The differences from hunting dogs are immediately noted—for instance, you cannot use a shock collar to train a fishing dog, "especially in salt water." The closest relation to hunting dogs that I could find in this path-breaking book are the gillie dogs, whose purpose is to "help the sport fisherman," though not precisely the way a good pointer can help a grouse hunter. Gillie dogs include such breeds as the floating mat dog, the logdog, the flounderhounder, the stringer spaniel, and the hatch-matching spaniel. You need not read far to appreciate that the author sure knows his dogs and fishing in great detail; this knowledge is, of course, crucial to a book like this.

One of the most interesting species are the dogfish dogs, which actually catch fish in ingenious ways. There are two kinds of dogfish dogs: those that sit and wait, like the blind John Milton, and those that actually pursue and catch fish. Of the dogfish dog, the author again stresses the advantage the breed has over hunting dogs, especially over "your regular terrestrial scoop-up-the-game dogs—mainly, they don't chase deer."

In the end, there is serious consideration given to the possibility of crossbreeding a batch of very special new dogs into one that would embody all the features of the best fishing dogs. This sounds terrifically promising.

I am reminded after reading this important break-through book that Amazon still lists J. R. Hartley's *Fly Fishing* as a serious personal account of a happy fly-fishing life, which too many American readers and reviewers found dull after it had been a hilarious bestselling spoof in England. At least one serious British writer read Ed Zern's delicious review of

Lady Chatterley's Lover (as the life of an English gamekeeper with "many passages on pheasant rearing, the apprehension of poachers, and the ways of controlling vermin that cannot take the place of J. R. Miller's *Practical Gamekeeping*") the way dumb Americans read D. H. Lawrence. Alas.

But I guess you'll have to make up your own mind about *Fishing Dogs*. Frankly, I found it a profound advancement of our knowledge about fishing and The Wonderful World of Dogs—and I intend to rush out and find me a well-trained and life-changing flounderhounder.

Nick Lyons
Woodstock, New York
October 2013

Introduction

It was thirty years ago yesterday that I discovered the fishing dogs. I know other people discovered them long before that. It was twenty years ago that I published the first ever book on fishing dogs. Since then, I've received hundreds of letters from people all over the world telling more about fishing dogs. They shared with me things I'd never heard or thought of—new uses for fishing dogs, how to train fishing dogs, new breeds of fishing dogs, and how to make a fishing dog. The biggest correspondence is from people who want to know if they make great pets and if they are registered with the AKC.

Somewhere in the midst of that deluge of letters, I decided I should update my previous book on fishing dogs. You might think it is because of all that new information that needs to be told, and partly that is true. But the bigger part is completely different.

Professor Coppinger discovers the fishing dogs.

I was going through my library in the dark and stumbled across the following book:

Richardson, Lieut.-Colonel Edwin Hautenville

Forty Years with Dogs

They forgot to put a date in the book, but my investigation centered on a picture of Mrs. Richardson in the frontispiece and it looks like she has an original Gucci handbag, which means it was published no earlier than 1921.

My copy is a blue-covered book that looks like it might have been damp for a number of years. I'd never heard of it, and certainly never read it, and *certainly* never met anyone who had. So I looked it up on the web and nearly dropped what teeth I have left—$750 USD. They said it was a rare book—so rare they didn't have a single review of it and invited me to review it. I told them I better not because the price might come down if people thought I'd actually read it.

Anyway, it set me to thinking and I realized that because of the sales, my first volume of *Fishing Dogs* is also a very rare book. Secondly, my book may also be getting a little pricy since nobody ever seemed to have read it. I realized that the time was right to revise, update, and rerelease *Fishing Dogs*, especially with the growing number of people interested in the fishing dogs, and *especially* those who see the marketing potential for these new kinds of dogs.

New breeds have sprung up (although it is very unlike these dogs to spring up). The number of people from the dog food industry who have talked to me about special diets is encouraging. And veterinarians are interested in the special medical problems these dogs have. The vet med companies have come up with powders and waterproof sprays to prevent leeches, water lice, and snails from attacking your fishing dog, for example.

Fishing dogs used to be just fishing dogs, meaning sportsperson's helpers, but now the breeders have taken a keen interest in them for other purposes. The demand for companion fishing dogs and pets has become enormous. Breeders have selected miniature fishing dogs the size of lily pads and gargantuan dogs that look like a weedy section of the Sargasso Sea. Many of these dogs are given to children who haven't even started to fish yet—the theory being that even though these dogs are very expensive and almost impossible to manage, pet ownership by children will foster a responsible ethic of outdoor activities.

So let us get to it and explore that wonderful world of dogs together.

Chapter 1

The Discovery of Fishing Dogs Thirty Years Ago

Very few of you will remember that thirty-some odd years ago, I decided I should try fishing. It was my midlife crisis (I'm over it now—midlife, that is) and fishing seemed like reasonably cheap therapy. There was this guy at the office, Stan, who is a fisherman, and I asked him if he'd teach me how to fish. He said, "Yes!" I thought that was generous of him at the time—but came to find out he couldn't seem to get a steady fishing buddy and wasn't getting any younger (which is as true now as it was then), and he was somewhat desperate.

Stan taught me some of the basics, like when you're in a boat in the middle of the pond, you cast toward the shore, and when you're on the shore, you cast toward the middle of the pond. It all made sense, and I quickly became a great fisherman, often bringing home little trophies that convinced my wife I was a good forager. Stan and I began to search for trophies together, and it wasn't long before we became fishing buddies.

"Fishing buddies" is an important concept. If you do catch-and-release fishing, for example, it is important to have someone trustworthy around to verify that you actually did release something. Trustworthiness is the foundation of male-to-male bonding. At its best, male-to-male bonding means that if your buddy sets his hook in your butt, he won't run off or pass out, but will remove the hook with a certain seriousness. It's okay to joke about it later when you tell all your friends what a good time you had, but the actual hook extraction scene happens with the silent formality of two men who know exactly what to do and what not to say.

There are two axioms in the institution of fishing buddies. The first is that good fishing buddies are hard to find. I once asked Stan if he'd ever had a fishing buddy before me, and he admitted that he'd fooled around a little bit, but never anything serious. I was kind of touched by this at the time, until I figured out the second axiom for myself: no fishing buddy is perfect, including Stan.

Stan's biggest problem is breakfast: he's committed to it, and it is always too big, too messy, and too late. His other big problem is knowing where to put things in the van. He packs objects according to when we will use them. The van-packing process should be like looking at life backwards: the first thing you want to use should be the last thing you pack. But Stan has the habit of packing first what we'll need right away. For example, he always wants to have breakfast before going fishing, and the breakfast stuff is under the fishing stuff, which is under the rainy-day stuff on clear days and right by the sunblock on rainy days. It's just not the way I like to run my life, that's all.

Unloading the van

Once we tried a trial separation. Stan went off to this far-away lake at five a.m. and sat in the local diner until these two old guys, seeing he was buddy-less, took pity on him and asked if he wanted to join them for the day. After several hours on the lake, according to Stan, one guy apologized for the other, who was not much of a fisherman and had in fact drifted off to sleep in the middle of a long cast. The guy told Stan that he was breaking in a new buddy because his old one had died, and he figured at his age he couldn't be all that fussy. It set Stan to thinking of that old expression, "After forty your chances of getting fulminated in an aluminum canoe are better than your chances of finding a good fishing buddy."

There was a lesson in that for both of us. During our trial separation, our wives suggested some professional counseling. One thing led to another, and our therapist suggested that maybe we should adopt a kid to take fishing with us. That seemed a little extreme to me, mainly because of the size of the boat, but when I suggested that we adopt a Swedish cook who actually liked peeling welded potato skins off the frying pan, or that we should limit our fishing to ponds behind all-night diners, everybody got mad at me.

Finally she (the therapist) suggested a dog. She wasn't all that experienced in counseling fishing buddies, but she'd had some success with childless couples and pets, and she thought it might work for us. I thought a dog might be a good solution: maybe a dog could at least get the burned home fries off the bottom of the pan. So I said I'd be willing to give it a try.

That is how we decided to get a fishing dog: a dog that would not only help us get our minds off one another's faults (like Stan's obsession for trying to find grass and lily pads before they are up in the early spring, just to mention one of his little hang-ups), but also help us with our fishing.

Stan, being the economist, said he'd pay for half the dog if I, the biologist, could find the right one. Since I was really into making this relationship work, I did some diligent research on fishing dogs. When I started my research, I didn't know real fishing dogs existed. Oh, I knew the dog paddle, but I mean breeds of dogs that do specialized tasks.

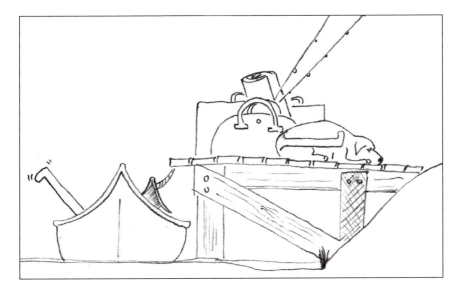

Dog paddle—collapsible

Being a scholar, I went first to the technical journals to see what other cultures had done in the way of breeding dogs to help with fishing. But because anthropologists focus their studies on "hunters and gatherers" and not "fishers and gatherers," they hadn't done any good studies. There were no good studies on fishing dogs until mine came out thirty years ago.

I quickly became amazed at how much had been written on hunting dogs, while almost nothing had been written on fishing dogs. Almost everything about these dogs is word-of-mouth. Eventually I talked to dozens of fishing sportspeople around the world about their fishing dogs and I was forced to come to this conclusion: you don't hear about fishing dogs because all the fishing dog types have been successful, and therefore there's no need to register them with the national kennel clubs.

Most hunting dog magazines are, first of all, full of advertisements about great dogs for sale—the best, the purest, the longest paper trail—and, second of all, articles about how to correct their faults, like how to stop them from chasing deer or eating the duck before delivering the carcass to hand.

Steadying your pointer so it doesn't chase the flushed bird is frequently written about. One of my favorite magazine subjects that comes up three times a year in *National Pointer* is "how to find your pointer." (Nothing can be worse than discovering, at the end of the day, that you're missing a dog—a dog *stuck on point*.) On the next page of the magazine will be an ad for the new and improved shock collar with the GPS attachment. Attaching GPS units to shock collars is the most brilliant advancement in training pointers since white bread. Now even lousy hunters know exactly where the dog is and can give the dog a little wake-up buzz. (Shock collars should never be used on fishing dogs—especially in salt water.)

Chapter 2

The First Fishing Dogs

I started my search for the elusive fishing dogs in England. There was a scholarly reason for that. The English have a long sporting history, a fascinating written history about sporting dogs. I know that the Germans, French, Italians, and Hungarians also have an equally long-written history about their sporting dogs, but I don't read German, French, Italian, or Hungarian. The Ethiopians have very little written about any kind of dogs, but I don't read Ethiopian either.

The first clue came in a fly shoppe (called tackle stores in America) when I was about to go on a salmon fish in Scotland. I asked the proprietor, a guy named Colin, what was hot, and without a blink, he said, "Collie dogs."

I could have fallen over backward. I practically gasped out a "What?"

"Well," he said apologetically, "if you don't want a collie dog perhaps you would prefer a yellow dog." I went for my bottle of heart pills. *Well, I'd found them* (the dogs, not the pills), I thought. I really had found fishing dogs! They existed! They weren't a figment of my imagination.

But I'm not quite so dumb, and, gaining my composure, I said almost nonchalantly, "Well let's take a look—you do have some?"

And he said with a big smile, "Oh yes, we have some really lovely ones."

My heart went pitter-patter as I anticipated buying my first half of a fishing dog. (I also kinda wondered whether Colin needed a fishing buddy.)

Colin walked briskly to a cabinet and brought down a glass-topped drawer . . . and there was a case of yellow and collie-black streamers—the black were all on the left and the yellow all on the right. (Because, he said with a twinkle, "They are all kept in alphabetical order.") They were kind of nice and sat up straight with their double-shafted hooks.

I practically screamed at poor Colin, "Those dogs are streamers!"

"Oh yes," he said with a smile of satisfaction, "These are the best dogs in all of Scotland." After years of study, I could believe him about that.

To make a really long and interesting story short—it was the Ghillie on the Gary (say it three times fast—it has a ring to it—Ghillie on the Gary) who was famous for tying flies from his dog's hair. Most of us realize that our dogs are a source for flies, but this guy brought a new wrinkle to that. Here was a guy who became famous for plucking the hair out of a dog and tying dry flies and streamers with it. He had a black (*collie* means black in Gaelic—comes from the word for coal) lab that sat on his right side and a yellow lab that sat on his left, which made perfect sense if you were facing him. The end of the long story was I bought a small package of *collie* and yellow dogs and was off on my very first fishing dog adventure. If there were two fishing dogs, there had to be more.

Fishing in Scotland was wonderful. Warm cozy evenings with the obligatory national drink, in a big sheepskin chair reading an old, obscure book. Therefore, some of my first leads on tracking down fishing dogs were literary, not exactly scientific. For instance, Lord Home[1] tells the story of an early relative of his (probably the guy they named the house after, even though we all know a Home is not a house). The earl was noted for landing a sixty-nine-and-a-half-pound salmon with his twenty-two-foot salmon rod and horsehair line. (Fly fishermen can probably back-order

---

[1] Home, Alec Douglas-Home, Baron. *Border Reflections, Chiefly on the Arts of Shooting and Fishing.* Illustrated by Rodger McPhail. London; Collins, 1979.

it from Orvis; I like Appaloosa myself.) Lord Home the
earlier . . .

> owned a dog that became notorious and then
> famous. It would sit on the riverbank at the mill
> stream opposite Wark castle, and in a morn-
> ing's fishing it would catch and land twenty
> or more salmon and lay them at its owner's
> feet. The jealous, humorless, and irate owner
> of the South Bank of the river brought a law-
> suit against the dog; the case was known as
> "Lord Tankerville versus a dog—the property
> of the Earl of Home." Much to the joy of the
> Scottish side, the dog won.

Lord Tankerville versus a Dog

Lord Home the later (but now, the late) also had a retriever
". . . which landed salmon by gripping them across the gills

and delivering them to hand." Herein was a clue; could it be that the Homes had a backyard strain of dogs that retrieved salmon naturally?

Think about it for a minute. You don't even have to be there to fish! Suppose there comes a day when you would like to go fishing, but for one reason or another, you have to stay home and mow the lawn. If you had a trained descendant of Lord Home's retriever, you could send him out by himself. Imagine the thrill of waiting at the door on a Saturday night, anxious to see just what luck he had.

Now suppose your fishing buddy couldn't go that day, either (cleaning windows). Then his dog could go with yours. You would have to make sure both dogs obeyed creel limits so they would have to be able to tell the difference between a smallmouth and a largemouth bass. (Of course, if your dogs were into catch-and-release, there would be no creel problem.)

If Home's retrievers had become a reality, fishermen could be judged by the quality of their dogs, just like other sportsmen. Hunters have the wintertime pleasure of seeing their gun and their deer heads mounted in mute splendor over the mantelpiece, while their retrievers lie curled up by the fire with their feet twitching. The best a catch-and-release fisherman can do is call his fishing buddy, who'd probably rather watch the Celtics game than hear again how I caught last summer's first fish, last fish, biggest fish, smallest fish, and most fish.

In any case, Lord Home's story was an inspiration to me in my research. Here again, if there was one dog that could retrieve and deliver salmon to hand, then there must be others that could help out with other fishing chores. It's like the dog paddle: practically everybody knows the dog paddle.

Dog paddle—self-portaging

The dog paddle is the most famous help to a fisherman, and it is often required that young sportspeople gain proficiency in it. It is so common that people out on the lake in an emergency will go instinctively for the dog paddle.

Dog paddle—puppies practicing

When I go anywhere near the water, I always have mine with me. Not only does the dog paddle propel you through the water, but it is self-portaging around rapids, a truly amazing combination. But, as far as I know, nobody has actually written: "The dog paddle is a self-propelling, fully independent locomotory system and everybody who goes near the water should have one and know how to use it." It should be the law!

As I'll demonstrate in this book, specialized breeds of fishing dogs, unlike the dog paddle, don't just happen. The evolution of each was slow, following a logical progression from an ancient form into the modern, highly specialized form. Since the early forms weren't any good, fishermen didn't notice them and therefore made no mention of them. But as centuries passed and the breeds evolved, getting better and better at their tasks, fishermen began to sit up and think about how to use and improve them.

This isn't surprising. The same kind of revelation happens with hunting dogs. How many times have you been sitting by the fire, reading a book, when a pack of coonhounds goes by under the window?

"What's that?" you say.

"Dogs," says the wife.

"Must be chasing a raccoon," you muse. "I didn't know we had coonhounds."

"I guess we do now," she says.

That's the way it is with evolution. You get up one morning, completely unsuspecting, and find somebody has discovered a new dog. And once you start looking for them, fishing dog breeds start bobbing up all over. This book is an attempt to put these discoveries in phylogenetic order and bring you up to date in The Wonderful World of Fishing Dogs.

There are some things people tend to lie about: their children, their cars, their dogs. Everybody's child is above average, everybody's car gets better gas mileage than mine, and everybody's dog is more intelligent than their kid. Well, fishing dogs really are worlds better than hunting dogs. I've searched the globe for the best and I don't think I'm stretching the truth on this.

You can dismiss this book as hypothetical if you want, but believe me, it is not. I wrote this book for the expert, the serious biologist and anthropologist—as well as for other fishermen interested in the bio-cultural evolution of man's best fishing friend. If parts of it seem farfetched to you, well, that's science.

Also, as Stan always says, "You can't please everybody"—and he should know.

Chapter 3

The Evolution of the Fishing Dogs

Because I'm a dog biologist, I have to start by explaining how we got the dogs in the first place. Most anthropologists now agree that dogs were the first domesticated animals[2] and they are descendants of captured wolf puppies. Some anthropologists believe the dog was the first step in the invention of civilization. In fact, there are those anthropologists who figure we wouldn't be civilized now if it wasn't for dogs that helped

[2] When it is said that most anthropologists agree, this does not mean they agree with each other. It simply means a preferential vote was taken on the question and dogs received the highest ranking even though nobody actually ranked them first. A couple of anthropologists actually tried using data, but it is difficult to use data and be democratic at the same time.

guard us against those terrible Neanderthals who were always lurking around like Yetis.

The first dog guarding against a Neanderthal.

Neanderthals were better hunters and got most of the wild game until the real humans adopted dogs and became bona fide hunters and gatherers. Dogs tipped the balance. The Neanderthal couldn't get enough to eat after the invention of dogs and went extinct. It was really a good thing because the geneticists now say that the Neanderthals had already started to fool around with those pretty little human girls. (We don't know if handsome human boys fooled around with Neanderthal girls, and we will never know because Neanderthals became extinct.) Neanderthals were a little like bears and chased what they wanted, but humans were more like wolves, which is why they got to domesticate wolves instead of bears—at the time, it was pretty clear that wolves wanted to become dogs and bears didn't.

However, hunters and gatherers lived all over the world at that time and they didn't all have dogs in the beginning. The ones who had dogs were better off and traveled a lot, following the herds, and evolved quickly into Hunter and Gatherer Gypsies (HGG). E.G. Walsh[3] says that gypsies continuously brought new breeds of dogs to Europe and Britain through the ages.

The problem was that the old-fashioned hunter and gatherers weren't doing so well as the HGGs and, evolution being what it is, they had to evolve into something else. The hunter-gatherers without dogs evolved fairly rapidly into farmers. It was a dramatic genetic change in that they received the gene for owning land. It finally ended up that the farmers owned all the land and the traveling gypsies had to stay on the roads between the farms.

That turned out to be very good for dogs. The gypsies started to breed all the useful dogs we have today. All the great hunting and working breeds of dogs were invented by the HGGs, and the farmers just got the strays that weren't good for anything except pets that barked a lot.

It was out of necessity that HGGs required off-the-road dogs that could go to places the gypsies weren't allowed and bring back food. At first, they developed the lurcher (the

---

[3]   Walsh, E.G., *Lurchers and Longdogs*. (Gloucestershire: Standfast Press Saul), 1977.

poacher's dog—a greyhound type, only better) that would sneak onto somebody's farm, catch rabbits, and bring them back to the road. But some rabbits were in holes and they found that they had to invent terriers to go dig them out so the lurcher could bring them back.

Well, it all went fine for a bit until the HGGs got sick of eating rabbit all the time and wanted to try something else, like deer. Now a lurcher or a terrier cannot carry a big animal back to the road. So the HGGs developed a great longdog that they called a deerhound. The deerhound would chase deer in circles and then onto the road, where the HGGs would be waiting. But then some really smart HGG discovered you could get sheep to come to the road the same way and bingo! The collies were invented. Many of us suspected that border collies were originally poachers' dogs because they seemed to be much better at herding somebody else's sheep than they are at your own.

There are conflicting theories of dog domestication, of course. Anthropology would not be what it is today if anybody had agreed on anything. Some still question whether dogs even came before or after farming. Those anthropologists who have actually tested the theory of raising wolf pups to be hunting dogs realize that early training methods for domesticating wolves into dogs required oakhoe handles or two-by-fours (*click* and *treat* came thousands of years later). Many anthropologists have suggested houses and gardens had to come before dogs, and not only because hoe handles suggest gardens and the two-by-four is synonymous with house building.

The big point is the dog domesticators needed somewhere to take the wolf pups once they removed them from the den. Most important for the domestication process was the need for wolf puppies to have a backyard where they could practice barking in order to become real dogs. Whichever version you believe, it should be clear that natural selection has favored dogs and barking, while two-by-fours and backyards have become noticeably smaller.

Hunters have spent a lot of time developing their dogs since the beginning. In fact, scientists now claim that hunters took the first wolf pups out of their dens more than ten thousand years ago and made them into hunting dogs. My field guide to the dogs lists 340 breeds of dog, and more than half of them (184, to be exact) are hunting breeds. That means hunters have developed one new breed of hunting dog every fifty years (10,000 ÷ 184) since that first Mesolithic hunter acquired that first wolf puppy.

(Part of the reason hunters have created so many breeds is that they have always known that if the new breed wasn't any good, they could register them with the AKC, where they make wonderfully beautiful show dogs and somewhat less wonderful pets.)

Realize that these hunters and gatherers were out there hunting and gathering all the time. And after they got the idea that there could be new breeds just waiting to evolve, they were looking in wolf dens for interestingly different kinds of wolf pups. Imagine a hunter's surprise, when, upon looking at a new den, he saw a short-legged wolf puppy. An enterprising hunter (which is rare, I know) would breed the short-legged puppy to some other hunter's short-legged puppy and they would just keep going until they finally got an animal that not only looked like a basset hound, but acted like a basset hound. Various cultures eventually came up with different ways of breeding dogs, some of which are discussed on the following pages.

BRITISH SYSTEM OF DOMESTICATING DOGS

Since the Victorian age, the British system of domesticating dogs has been based on the principle of natural selection, first written about by Al Wallace (1823–1913) in England in 1858. Another Englishman, Charlie Darwin (1809–1882), worked out the details in 1859. When the principle of natural selection is applied to domestic animals, especially dogs, it is called *unnatural selection*. This is certainly obvious in the cases of the basset hound and the shar-pei.

The Wallaceo–Darwinian system of breeding dogs by unnatural selection is well over a hundred and fifty years old now and is holding up pretty well in England. It is such a terribly slow process that the English have developed very few breeds of dogs. Embarrassingly, the English haven't done as well as normal hunters in developing new dogs. It would appear to be that the evolution of a lot of new terriers has simply come about through breeders giving old breeds different names, thus making up "new" breeds all the time They've done a nice job preserving the famous HGG border collie. By the clever use of unnatural selection, they have made all border collies the same size and color while preserving their sheep-stealing gait. And, of course, there's the old English sheepdog. The Brits, knowing how long it takes to breed up a good dog, called this new breed olde Englishe sheepdogge right from the start. But as the great manor houses were turned into museums or otherwise fell into disrepair, what was left of breeding the best for the best was neglected and forgotten. The old stock was turned over to the kennel clubs, which had substituted the Quasimodo principle (only breed to the weird ones) for tedious natural selection. The English bulldog is a good example of how quickly the Quasimodo principle has brought British dog breeding up to speed.

FRENCH SYSTEM OF DOMESTICATING DOGS

The basset hound is not an American breed, or even British, and as Mark Twain would say, not even a Christian breed, but rather it's French. In France, they have a very effective system of evolution working for them, and they have developed many different breeds. The French System was the brainchild of Jean-Baptiste Pierre Antoine de Monet, Chevalier de Lamarck (1744–1829). It is called the *theory of inheritance of acquired characteristics.*

Lamarck believed that an organism passes on to its off-spring those characteristics that help it survive. On their way to becoming bassets, wolves could pass on their short-leggedness to their offspring by setting a good example while they were alive. In other words, if wolves worked hard to get ahead, and acquired short legs, then they could leave those legs to their puppies. Thus, one didn't have to wait around a long time for basset hounds, as one does now.

Lamarck theorized that wolves were sick of living in the wild (especially as there was less and less wild all the time in France). He felt that, in fact, wolves really wanted to be dogs. And as most of us learned from our mothers, "you can be anything you want to if you want it enough." Wolves simply had to start behaving the way they wanted to look and they soon started to look the way they were behaving, thus evolving into the 340 (so far) breeds of dog. The process still works today.

A simple example will suffice. As many of you already know, dogs have a great desire to please their masters, and their masters reward this desire. Thus, if a dog is behaving like a beagle, but looks like an Irish setter, then the owner is displeased with the dog because he thinks that a dog that looks like an Irish setter should be acting like an Irish setter. Since it is acting like a beagle, then it is misbehaving and needs to be disciplined. Of course, even if it were acting like an Irish setter, it might still be disciplined, because no dog should want to please its master by acting like an Irish setter.

It is impossible to know which breed of hunting dog early man had in mind when he trained the first domesticated wolf pups. That means the wolf pups didn't know at first what they were supposed to look like or who they were supposed to please. The problem was further complicated by the fact that early man didn't know what dogs were supposed to look like nor did early man know a lot about hunting (which has remained true to the present time). That means they didn't know what the different breeds were going to turn out to be, so they didn't know if the wolf puppies were behaving properly. Since the wolf pups were going to turn into 184 different breeds of hunting dogs alone, then it must have been really confusing for the domesticators to know which one they were working on at any given time. No doubt this is why so many bird dogs chase deer.

In scientific terms, chasing deer is a displacement activity. A displacement activity is something you do to look busy when you don't really know what you should be doing—and if you don't know what you're doing, how on earth would you know what to look like? So the general rule for hunting dogs is: if you don't know what you're doing, displace a deer.

GERMAN SYSTEM OF DOMESTICATING DOGS

The Germans have their own system of breeding dogs and are the only people who are still actively producing new working breeds of dog. While the English are still trying to perfect their existing breeds by continuing with unnatural selection and still have a long way to go, and the French are still trying to find names for the breeds that are trying to be real dogs, the Germans methodically create registered, brand-name dogs at a regular rate. The German shepherd and the Doberman pinscher are just two of their recent creations.

The Germans invent new dogs by averaging out older breeds. All individuals of a breed make up an average of the breed, which then makes up the standard. Look at it this way: somewhere there is a vision of the perfect dog and it is described in the breed standard. Since the average of all the dogs within a breed is a theoretical number, there may not be a single dog that represents that average. What that means is that at any given time there is no such thing as a perfect dog. That should be pretty obvious.

Statistically speaking, the average is called the mean, $\bar{x}$, and in German that will be clear. The Germans crossbreed two or more different purebreds, which are close approximations of the theoretical average mean, which then emerges as a totally new average, never seen before. Crossbreeding always produces a new mean, something known as statistically bizarre. Some breeders cross the crosses and get a thoroughly mean breed. The standard deviations are difficult to calculate, but some believe that surely the Rottweiler is a good example.

Like all of us, the Germans are concerned with breed purity, thus they breed only purebred dogs to other purebred dogs, even if the crosses started out pure, to develop totally new purebred dogs: a dog representing the average, or mean, of the parents. In scientific terms, it is called blending inheritance. Take the (Doberman) pinscher, for example. Herr (Mr.) Ludwig Dobermann was a tax collector in the 1860s. To protect himself, Lud created a truly mean dog by breeding purebred great Danes with purebred German shepherds,[4] plus a little purebred Rottweiler, some purebred beauceron,[5] and a touch of purebred English greyhound.[6]

There is more to the story, which the Germans freely admit. German is such a difficult language, it was practically impossible to write it all down. So the recipes telling how much of each breed to put into the blender to create the new breed again has been lost. It is now impossible to recreate a Doberman from the beginning and we have to stick with the one we have. Only by breeding Dobermans to Dobermans can we preserve the original proportions and have conservation of the original, which has become very important in keeping Dobermans up to standard.

---

[4] The purebred German shepherd itself was originally created by breeding together all the purebred sheep herding and sheep guarding dogs west of the Urals and then allowing them to mate spontaneously with purebred wolves.

[5] A French wolf that wanted to be a sheepdog—lots of wolves want to be sheepdogs because it is easier to get close to sheep if you're a sheepdog.

[6] Greyhounds from England were borrowed from the Egyptians long before the English learned about unnatural selection.

ITALIAN SYSTEM OF DOMESTICATING DOGS

The Italian system is one of the quickest and most practical systems of dog development in the world: you don't actually do any breeding at all. Simply take any dog and name it after a vegetable. Follow the dog around until it finds the vegetable, and pesto!—a virtual transmogrification—you have a new breed. The most famous example is the truffle hound. A few years ago, people in Italy were following little mongrel dogs around as the dogs looked for the mushrooms they were named after. Because they named a lot of dogs truffle hounds, they ceased being mongrels and became real truffle hounds.

Well, some of them became real truffle hounds, but a lot of them were not very good. The Italians have saved these not-so-good dogs from extinction by registering them with the Italian Kennel Club. Now anyone can own a purebred registered truffle hound and keep it strictly as a pet and be guaranteed it won't wander off looking for truffles. There are mixed opinions on just how bad they are. Some say that because they are only registered with the Italian Kennel Club, they couldn't be too bad. That may change, however, because the Americans are trying to get them registered. The breed literature seems to indicate that they're not *too* bad. For example, the breed standard says, "They make good show dogs and not so good pets." So they are not all bad and there is hope for them.

The big breakthrough for the Italians was developing the universal system for training dogs. Training truffle hounds is a perfect example of the Italian ingenuity. You buy truffle-scented olive oil and inject it into a tennis ball. Let your truffle-aspiring puppy chew on the tennis ball. When it becomes bigger (the puppy, not the tennis ball) you throw the tennis ball and play fetch-it-up, then you bury the tennis ball when the dog isn't looking and let it dig it up. Then when the dog is looking, you pretend to throw the ball to where it is really buried—the rest is history. This is called *positivo condiccione* in Italian.

The Italians have developed several breeds by using the tennis-ball technique. For example, since molasses is reasonable easy to inject into a tennis ball, they invented the Neapolitan molasses dog in one generation, quickly followed by broccolio Italiano and the chili con cani. The one that was harder was spumoni Italiano. which tracks ice cream, and which came only recently with the invention of thermos balls.

Most of these dogs have all been big losers and had to be registered with the Italian Kennel Club to save them.

NORTH AMERICAN SYSTEM OF DOMESTICATING DOGS[7]

For the most part, Americans have not been very creative about making new breeds of dogs. Mostly what they do is change

---

[7] See the French-Canadian system of domesticating dogs for a minority-supported method.

the names of European breeds. So you get the American fox hound, the American pit bull terrier, the America Staffordshire terrier, and the American water spaniel, all of which were breeds somewhere else before they became "all American." *Oh!* you say, *what about the Alaskan malamute??* What about it! They evolved into dogs when Alaska was still owned by the Russians, so technically they are Russian dogs. And the Russians want them back, and if nobody minds, they should have them all. It's the least we could do for them.

Americans will do anything to make people think they are creating new breeds. The most inventive method is naming dogs that wash ashore from sinking ships—obviously a new breed, even though nobody knows where they came from. The Chesapeake Bay retriever is a nice example. There is also the cover-your-butt new breed: some Beacon Hill Brahmin has an accidental breeding between a French bulldog and a local boxer and calls the puppies Boston terriers, which is a new mean average.

I say most Americans aren't clever dog inventors. That is because most Americans are not coon hunters. From looking at a list of American dogs, you would have to agree that hound men are the most imaginative and inventive dog breeders in the whole world! There are 185 breeds of coon dogs in America (too many to list them all here), which is one more breed than all of the rest of hunting dogs combined. And from what I have seen, every one of those breeds wanted to be "nothing but a hound dog crying all the time."

The other noteworthy feature about coonhounds is that almost all of them have been successful because very few have been registered. How they ever got all those different breeds to hunt one species, the raccoon, is beyond me. In fact, there is a dilemma here. If these dogs are so good, how come the raccoon population keeps growing?

Most Americans are of the opinion that all the breeds have already been created and the breeder's job is to preserve them, improve them, and make sure they get registered. To change a breed or adapt it to a new use is sacrilegious. In their view, there is one perfect shape for each breed. The American dog breeder's goal is to have all the individual dogs in each breed look like the perfect dog. The breeders have written standards, which are guides to recognizing those perfect dogs. Breeders are so passionate about their work that we have hardly any bad-looking dogs in America. Each year, the show judges look over all the dogs and pick the one that embodies perfection, entitling him to commit original sin with the dozens of slightly-less-than-perfect dogs, thereby achieving an average improvement. The goal of the American dog movement is to have all members of a breed look alike. How they act is not so high on the list.

Chapter 4

Classification of Fishing Dogs

The first system of classifying hunting dogs was developed by the early Greeks, who grouped dogs according to the four known basic elements: Earth, Air, Fire, and Water. Many dog-breeding hunters stuck to the Greek system and named their breeds after the medium in which the dogs worked. Thus you have dogs that hunt in the Water (the Chesapeake Bay retriever, for example); inside the Earth (terriers); in Fire (only the Dalmatian survives to the present, probably because it was wise enough to follow the fire truck rather than snuffling about in the flames); and, of course, the Airedale.

One modern way of classifying dogs is by their function. Hunting dogs whose names often reflect their purpose include staghounds, foxhounds, wolfhounds, and lion hounds (these last are extremely rare). But sometimes the nomenclature within a class gets murky, and you quickly find you cannot rely on dogs' names to reveal accurately what their domesticator had in mind. Take the terriers as an example. Terriers (the name comes from the Latin word for earth, *terra,* which surprised me because when I started this research I didn't know that hunters even knew Latin) go after prey in holes in the ground. The specialty of many terrier breeds is rodents and other vermin, and indeed some are named properly like the rat terriers or fox terriers, in order to keep a certain consistency of terminology within the terrier group. For example, fox terriers go into holes or underground dens after foxes, so they are aptly named. Likewise, a foxhound avoids holes and looks specifically above the ground for specifically foxes.

But don't conclude that hound breeders, at least, have figured out how to name their breeds: think of truffle hounds. Their job is to dig into the ground for fancy mushrooms, and therefore they should be known as truffle terriers. If they specialized in *chasing* the mushrooms, then they could be called truffle hounds.

Another system of classifying hunting dogs is by size. This differentiation often comes within a given breed. Poodles, for example, descended from an ancient and *highly* talented French duck-retrieving dog (Brigitte barbet), and are classified as standard (large), miniature (small), or toy (even smaller than that). Beagles, whose name supposedly means "to bay from the throat"[8] and who are noted for baying from the throat after rabbits, also come in different sizes. You can have the 15-inch (38-cm) beagle, the 10-inch (25.4-cm) beagle, or the small bore (9-mm) beagle.

Still other hunting breeds have regional names—like Labrador retriever, Karelian bear dogs, Nova Scotia duck tollers, or Boston terriers. And then there are dogs that people modestly named after themselves: the monks of St. Hubert developed the St. Hubert hound; the Reverend Jack Russell crafted his own terrier. Since they named the breeds after themselves, who knows what the dogs were supposed to do? It would not surprise me if many of you assume that the little Jack Russell terrier ran around looking in holes for His Reverence.

To further confuse the nomenclature issue, many hunting dogs perform tasks other than the one they were bred for. Pointers, for example, can be trained to retrieve. It is easy to get bird retrievers to chase deer and deerhounds to hunt porcupines. My wife had a Chessie, a fine duck-retrieving dog, but the dog preferred to scarf blueberries right from the bush. She (the dog) was a top-notch blueberry hunter. Unfortunately, she (my wife) could not get her dog to "deliver to bucket," and most of the blueberries were eaten by the dog. (The rest were useful for

---

[8]   "Beagle" is not related to "bugle," in spite of orthographic and sonorous similarities; "bugle" is apparently, and inexplicably, related to the Latin word for a baby ox, *buculus*.

staining rugs.) If she lived in Italy, she probably could have the thrill of registering her dog as a Blueberry Hill Hound.

So, really, unless you know the breed, you have no way of knowing, based on its name, what the dog does. Does the Kerry blue terrier's name indicate its emotional state? Is an Irish water dog supposed to fetch a chaser?

Major Digression

I know I am getting too technical and some think I have lost the Plott. What is a dog supposed to do regardless of what it is called? One might ask: what is the real function of a dog? The first thing every book on dogs says is the dog was domesticated to help man, so let us take a minute to see how hunting dogs help man.

I have been working on a study of the energetics of hunting and fishing with dogs. Many people say that "man domesticated wolves so they could be hunting companions." First question a real anthropologist would ask is: what does *hunting companion* mean? The bigger question: is the hunting of anything with dogs worth it? If you go out into the forest with a dog or dogs and hunt, skin, kill, and eat some smelly thing, will you get back the same or more calories that you and the dog consumed in the first place? Darwin says is the benefit of hunting has got to be greater than the expense of hunting, otherwise you will go extinct.

Recently I went to the Okefenokee Swamp part of Florida/Georgia to test the benefit of hunting hogs divided by the cost of hunting hogs with specially selected and trained Plott hounds. I divided the study into seven testable categories based on the long tradition observed by hog hunters hunting wild hogs with Plott hounds. These seven traditions are traceable by certifiable anthropologists all the way back to the early Neolithic.

These traditions are as follows:

First—get up at 3 a.m. and load dogs into a beautiful four-door, four-wheel-drive pickup truck with cable winch and special crates for dogs. The reason for getting up so early was discovered years ago by David Harcombe[9] who says ". . . get on the road as soon as possible with a stop for breakfast at a popular early morning café." The purpose of getting up early was to beat the crowd to the restaurant and get a good table for breakfast.

After breakfast, drive two hours to the hunt club reserve. Upon arriving, discover you have forgotten the key to the gate. Call Georgia friends and tell them if they will bring a key, they can go hunting with you. Two more pickups come within the hour with more hunters and dogs. Finally open the gate.

---

[9]   David Harcombe, *Early Starts*, Earthdog-Running Dog #243, Oct. 2012.

Second—Drive on swamp roads along the edge (sometimes off the edge, getting stuck) of the Okefenokee Swamp. Two more trucks join us there. Estimated value of the pickups is approaching a quarter of a million dollars and going up by the hour. Look for fresh hog tracks by driving along wilderness roads where whole corn was spread the night before.

Third—Find fresh tracks, and let loose one to three dogs per truck (approximately eight) on the trail. The dogs run into the swamp often in different directions, either bawling or chopping (technical terms for baying and yodeling). Each dog is equipped with four collars: GPS, telemetry, shock collar, and name tag collar. Breeders are trying to select dogs with longer necks. Many hunters can't wait for evolution to work and have gone

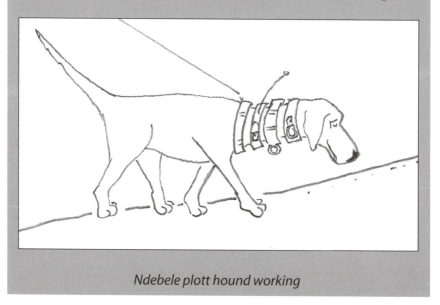

Ndebele plott hound working

to neck stretching procedures as the need for more collars grows. There are two basic techniques for stretching Plott necks: the first (the one I like best uses the coil methods of the Giraffe Necked Women of Thailand) and the second and simpler system employed by the Ndebele tribe of South Africa.

Fourth—(This is the main part of the hunt.) All the hunters talk together at the trucks about where the dogs might have gone. Sometimes everybody jumps in the trucks and drives in different directions while talking on CB radios 10/4. At the end of the day, everybody drives up and down the roads using triangulating telemetry methodologies, GPS devices, or—as a last resort—they shock the dogs and listen for yelps.

Fifth—Each truck tries to capture as many dogs as possible, catching them one at a time. Meet other trucks at a predefined location and get your own dogs back and give others their dogs back until everybody has the same number of dogs they started with. Now it is time to drive home and the last driver out locks the gate, making positively sure nobody is locked in.

Sixth—Gas up the pickup trucks and get ice cream on the way home.

Seventh—Get home, drink whiskey, and analyze the hunt. Compare it to past hunts and make plans for future hunts.

I'm sure it was the same in ancient times, and I've seen pictographs on the walls of the pyramids where the only difference was horses instead of pickup trucks. That makes you sit up and think—maybe horses had to come before hunting with dogs. Certainly talking had to come even before that.

Long ago in ancient China, when the population was very low, the Chinese hunted with dogs. Then they discovered it made more energetic sense to eat the dogs at home and not go anywhere. Now they have a great big human population.

Now that you have a better idea of what dogs do, it will be easier for you to understand how the breeding and naming of hunting dogs works. This will enable you to interpolate all this information as we get into the more complex subject of the fishing dogs. Problem is nobody had classified the fishing dogs until I made the first attempt thirty years ago. At that time, how many of the 184 breeds of hunting dogs were fish-hunting dogs? Only four. Fishing dogs are extremely quiet animals; it simply serves no useful function to bark in or under water and, therefore, they do not come to the public's attention like the tree-bayers.

The four breeds of fishing dog that managed to get listed in the field guide were really only token fishing dogs. The Portuguese water dog chases fish that escape from the nets of fishermen and brings them back. This commercial application generally bars them from sporting events. The Labrador retriever purportedly helps fishermen draw in nets, but to tell the truth. I have never seen it done. The beagle is included in this group on the strength of its use "even for catching fish," but this assertion strikes me as a sales gimmick or hopeful afterthought. The only beagle I ever knew that caught fish was one that fell through the ice: we found him the next summer full of eels. And, in Japan, the Kyūshū dog is noted as a "fisherman's helper." We'll see what that means in the section on bilge dogs.

There are actually many more fishing breeds, dogs which far outclass these four in piscatorial abilities. Fishermen have always been interested in perfection, and they improve on what they have that is good, rather than casting about for new models. For that reason they have not saturated the field with dogs to the extent that hunters have. Any less-than-perfect fishing dogs are rigorously selected against, which is in stark contrast to hunting dogs, which are simply left home to keep the hearth warm if they don't work well. (You would never hear of a pike pointer, for example, getting stuck on a point.)

Hunters developed two kinds of dogs: helper dogs are typified as the old dog that drags himself to his feet when the hunting jacket comes off the peg and accompanies his master to the store for cigars; participatory dogs are primarily deer (or coon) chasers.

Fishermen have also developed two types of dog, both of which are unique to fishing. Gillie dogs are like tools: fishermen use them to increase their chances of hooking a fish. Fish spotter dogs actually participate in the fish, just as a pointer participates in the hunt. To simplify things (and because I can), I've chosen a classification system for the fishing dogs that is based on their function in relation to fishermen.

Chapter 5

Introduction to the Gillie Dogs

The gillie dogs are simply dogs that help the sport's fishermen. Within the gillie class, there are three types: 1) the baildales, which work inside the boat and which evolved from the ancestral bilge pups into the Pacific monsoon dog, the Greek gyro, and the various bowplunk dogs, including the storied Maine bow dog; 2) the already-bailed-dales, which do their work outside the boat and include such breeds as the floating mat dog, the logdog, the flounderhounder, the stringer spaniel and the hatch-matching spaniel, and 3) a subfamily of the already-bailed-dales, the dogfish, including breeds like the angler dog, the tippups, the χ-nooky, and the sealyhams.

Small Digression: About Gillies

In Great Britain, or better yet Scotland, a *gillie* (or ghillie, or the archaic ghylly) is a sportsman's helper. Long before Scotch-drinking sportsmen and other partygoers thought up the designated driver, the ancient Scots always designated a person who specialized in carrying their clan's chief across rivers on his back.

A ravine or glen in Scotland is a *gill* and pronounced *ghill* by a Scotsman. (In Gaelic the "h" is never silent because of the climate.) The carrier was the ghylly, but the root of that word is *gille,* which comes from the Gaelic word *gille,* which means boy or lad or laddie in ancient English. The carryee was simply known as Chief or, when in formal dress, Sir Chief. A good gillie would lift weights (e.g., toss the caber) in his off hours to stay in shape, because throughout the years, chiefs got bigger and bigger (we can determine this by comparing suits of armor from the past and the present). A good gillie would also practice keeping the chief's feet out of the water (so his shoes wouldn't rust) and avoid slimy rocks; it was very important not to drop the chief, and even little slips might warrant a cuff behind the ear.

Legend has it that once upon a time, a chief was being carried across a nice gill and, spotting an early sea-run salmon, he asked his gillie to "holde ye stille, ghylly, that I might fishe the ghill fore ae whylle." It was this chief, sitting on the gillie's back, whipping the old horse-hair back and forth, who gave the word *gillie* its modern meaning. Since then, the British have used the term to mean a sportsman's helper. You often see these gillies on Scottish riverbanks, dressed in tweeds (commonly, a three-piece woolen suit), tying flies to match the hatch for gentlemen dressed in waders, waterproof woolen sweaters, and a snappy little woolen caps, who are whipping flies at the end of a seven-weight line at passing salmon, which are on a spawning run and therefore not feeding. The gillie on the Gary is a perfect example of such a helper, although he may also have been the first dog plucker.

Chapter 6

Bilge Pups

FOUNDING STOCK

When I was researching bilge pups, I had a shocker. *Shocker* is a technical scholarly term: when you are researching something and discover something else, something unsuspected, that something else is a shocker. As you may have noticed, I try to bury my research shockers in the middle of paragraphs so only the most pedestrian of readers will note them. And you might note that this is the longest paragraph in the book, thus the shocker comes after most people have given up trying to figure out what the paragraph is about and forgotten what the topic sentence was. The shocker is: Our ancestors ate dogs! That was in the period before they became "man's best friend," which happened much later, according to historians. It's too bad, but everybody's ancestors ate dogs, unless somebody's ancestors (like turtles) were vegetarians all the way down.

At first I thought I was misreading the ancient literature when I came across, "These marineating dogs would become available if someone needed a snack" or "It is time to chow down." Often the references to dog-eating are stated innocuously, even euphemistically, like, "Bilge pups went to sea in little vessels of their own," or, "Sushihounds (a Japanese bilge pup breed) helped with lunch." The eating of dogs is a sad fact, but it is also the cornerstone of the dog's evolution, as I shall explain.[10]

The first written records of these ancient fishing dogs were in the log books of ancient Chinese fishing boats. Fishermen

---

[10] The reason we don't eat dogs anymore is that only the inedible ones survived long enough to reproduce. This is a wonderful example of Darwinian evolution in action: natural selection has favored the smelliest breeds, which people would find repulsive to eat. If you don't believe this theory, test it by asking somebody if they would like chicken in a basset, or baked Alaska husky for supper. The immediate response will be, "That's disgusting." And I agree. I can't think of a single breed that is edible anymore—except maybe German shepherd pie.

Helping with lunch

sailed out for extended periods, so they stowed lots of junk food down in the bilge, and it was there that they began breeding bilge pups in quantity. Junk chandleries were the original puppy mills. The Chinese were also the first to wok their dogs.

Sad fact or not, being eaten has changed many organisms into something useful. That is the basis of evolution. Bilge pups radiated into useful breeds in two distinct ways: 1) the evolutionary survivors were distasteful, and inedible, which gave them survival value and opportunities to be useful; 2) dogs that were accidently pumped from the boat during bilging, or released during a shipwreck, were pre-adapted to already-bailed-dales conditions and floated effortlessly around the world, finally washing up on beaches and in bayous where, in those days, there were not as many people to eat them. Thus, for them, not being eaten is not a product of natural selection, but an acquired characteristic (see discussion about Lamarck, page 23).

The evolutionary problems for these washouts were staggering (remember "survival of the fittest") and it is a wonder that they have become so important in the advancement of new breeds. It is thought that the way to get really good dogs is to breed the best to the best, but there were no descendants of really good sushies. The most logical explanation is to assume that only the worst sushies lived long enough to breed and so the ancients bred the worst to the worst. That in itself may explain we have such trouble with many modern breeds.

Like so many breeds of dog, bilge pups are named for the region they come from. Imagine for a minute the bilge of an ancient boat. My goodness, it must have been beautiful down in the dark oily depths of an ancient scow: a placid pool of carbon-based sludge enriched with nutritious gurries[11] and protected from the rough seas of the outside world. Here, in short, was the perfect evolutionary environment: rich in raw materials, climatically stable, and geographically and genetically isolated from the rest of the world—a niche so to speak. These are the ingredients for evolution. This is the place Darwin was looking for as he sailed around the globe in the good ship *Beagle* in search of the origin of species. And yet, there it was, traveling along a few meters below him: the primordial soup of dogs. The *Beagle* is one of science's great ironies.

---

[11] Gurry is fish offal, a highly descriptive term.

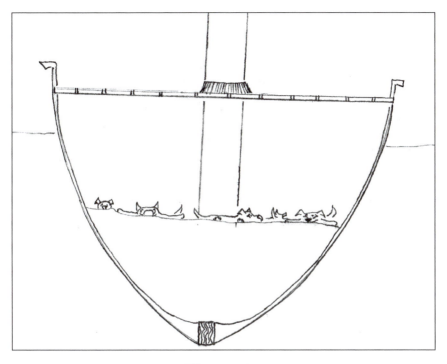

Bilge puppies

Throughout the years, of course, the bilge pups quietly evolved. Mostly, they changed color, where the most ancient color—the standard chocolate cream pie shade that typifies several modern dog breeds—died out.[12] The reason for this was not that ships' cooks preferred the flavor of chocolate-colored dogs—quite the contrary. When they reached into the dark

---

[12]   Chocolate is an example of what biologists call *cryptic coloration:* it blends in with its environment. Chocolate is so tasty that if it *could* be seen in the dark, it would be completely wiped out by now. This is why so many people trip over chocolate labs in the dark. Those bilge pups that were conspicuous ended up investing all their energy in lunch programs and had none left for reproductive success. But colors like mocha fudge, coffee merle, walnut brindle, marbled pecan, and black-and-tan were not readily visible to ancient seafarers, which is why these bilge colors survived and are so popular among dog fanciers today.

bilge to get a dog for lunch, the lighter-colored, vanilla-coated dogs naturally came first to the eye. Eventually the vanilla bilge pup population died out from over-predation by ships' cooks.

Thus the darker tops and lighter underneaths of the successfully adapted dogs exemplified the same principle as fish coloration (the dark color of the river bottom on top of the fish and the light color of the sky underneath). When the cook looked down into the dark hold, the dark underbelly of the bilge pups was indistinguishable from the ship's bottom, whereas if the cook was under the dog looking up, the dog's bottom looked more like the sky looks if you're looking at it through bilge water. The next time you see a German shepherd, ask yourself why it has a black pattern on top and a tan pattern on the bottom. Really, it could have been the other way around and shepherds could be lighter colors on top and have black bellies. Think on it.

Because of this increasingly effective camouflage coloration, centuries passed when less and less was known about these hidden dogs in our lives. But evolution was taking place. It always does. You can't stop it. Aside from the dark color, another trait naturally selected was short legs: bilgies didn't need legs. They didn't need much of anything but a heads-up attitude and a buoyant disposition.

Chapter 7

Baildales

As populations of bilge pups increased (ah, yes, there is hanky-panky and rumpy-pumpy going on in the bilge), and competition (the battle of the bilge) for the little morsels from above, evolution might easily have led the pups to a more aggressive, shark-like nature. Bilge pups could have developed pack behaviors homologous to those of their wolf ancestors—behaviors which, coupled with their aquatic lie-in-wait hunting techniques, they might have used to torpedo some unsuspecting merchant mariner who ventured into the bowels of the ship and, inevitably, into the bowels of the dogs. But these are just dogs, and dogs have to be taught to be mean. All dogs, even the edible kind, are innately cuddly.[13]

---

[13] I don't know why bilge pups never became popular as pets, and since they don't actually do anything, neither do I understand why they haven't been registered with the AKC.

Besides, these bilge pups were survivors. To eat an ancient mariner would be to the dog's disadvantage: who would sail the ship? Their emerging and mutually beneficial symbiotic relationship with man was centered on keeping the bilge clean. Well, not exactly clean, but different, and better. Eventually they became gillie dogs. The helping behaviors perfected by the bilge pups involved getting water out of the boat, thus the category name of these modern gillie breeds: bail(s)dale(s).[14]

Baildales are a general functional category, which can be compared with other differentiations of dogs such as the working or sporting dog. Each of these categories is divided into subgroups, which are again subdivided. For example, one subgroup of the category working dog is the sheepdog, which comprise the conducting dogs (dogs that chase sheep from place to place) and the non-conducting sheepdogs (dogs that lie around the farm and bark a lot). In each of these subgroups, there are several breeds; e.g., border collies, great Pyrenees, and Catahoula leopard cowhog dogs.[15]

---

[14] Etymological note: breeders of baildales have split into different camps over a linguistic point. Some use the plural *bailsdale*, while others (like me) anglicize the word by simply adding an *s,* thus *baildales*. Still others adopt the Hungarian plural and write *baildailok* (dropping the final-*e* and inserting the pluralizing-*ok*), the way komondor(ok) and kuvasz(ok) breeders do (but then journalists, with great logic but little Hungarian orthographic knowledge, call them *komondoroks* and *kuvaszoks,* which is a double plural, and I don't think the AKC accepts such hybrids, which is okay by me).

[15] Just because you never heard of Catahoula leopard cowhog dogs doesn't mean the breed doesn't exist. Look it up.

Within the baildale category are subgroups, all of which we think are descended from the ancient bilgies. They have one trait in common: they all gillie from inside the boat. Later, I will contrast them with the already-bailed-dales that also descended from the bilge pups, but they gillie from *outside* the boat. And then there are the dogfish, which are a different category altogether.

First, let's look at why baildale behavior was needed. The original fishermen used the waterlog, a style of boat that actually got better with age. After many years in the water, the internal portion of the log would rot away, leaving only the outside. Since they were already saturated, waterlogs were the only vessel ever invented that didn't leak. Still, they evolved, eventually, into the canoe, and the evolution of the canoe was simultaneous with that of the leak. Since then, the leak has become standard equipment on all boats.

With the perfection of the leak, boats were increasingly able to ship water.[16] Boat owners who shipped too much water were selected against, and so, naturally, were their bilge pups. I'm sure you can see where this is going: any mutations that led to the survival of boating humans also led to the survival of boating dogs. Most of the time, these symbiotic mutations were the responsibility of the dogs, which developed two methodologies: monsooning, which rids the boat of excess water,

---

[16] Shipping water is a nautical expression meaning to take water from one place to another by boat.

Evolution of the canoe

and ballasting, which prevents the boat owner from bringing in too much water. As time went on, each behavior led to specialization of tasks, and two main sub-subgroups of baildales evolved: the monsoon dogs and the ballast dogs.

Monsoon Dogs

A single gene mutation changed the edible bilge puppy into a monsoon dog. This was the first mutation that transformed the archaic proto-dog (bilge pups) into modern dogs as we know them today. This was the original mutation that changed dogs from just something to eat into to "man's best friend." There couldn't be a more important mutation in the evolution of the symbiotic relationship between man and dog. This mutation has survived through thousands of years of evolutionary history to all the presently existing breeds except the Mexican hairless, the only dog to have completely lost it.

The resulting monsoon gene imparts a functional behavioral perfection to this breed that was highly valued by mariners through the ages, so much so that these genes were dispersed throughout the whole dog world and are now virtually ubiquitous, albeit vestigial, in hunting and other nonworking breeds.

Monsoon dogs lie in the bilge of a boat until they are disturbed by the shipping of water. When the water reaches nose level,

Monsoon dog—pre-monsooning (page 57) and monsooning behavior

which is their high water mark, the dog instinctively rises up out of the bilge (think about the creature from the lost lagoon) and unleashes with tremendous power a series of epicentric rotational reciprocations, expelling boat-threatening waters over the side.

Monsooner Breed Standards

Once, dogs had hair all around their bodies, but this is a fault in the monsoon breed. Water absorbed by primitive chest and belly hair simply goes back into the boat during reciprocations, which is energetically inefficient. Careful breeding and natural selection among the original monsooners favored dogs with little or no abdominal hair; also, the hairless stomach characteristic of most modern dogs is vestigial, meaning that if you look at your dog's tummy, you won't see any hair and you won't know why (unless you've read this book).

Certain passages in ancient literature seem to imply that the original monsoon dogs could rid a boat of five ewers of water in a single shake. Field trial records are, unfortunately, unavailable, having been lost (or perhaps stolen by disgruntled breed club secretaries). It is an age-old tradition in dog breeding to lose the breed records, so the dogs' attributes live on in delightfully unreliable oral traditions and dog breeds attain a status closely supported by cultural mythology (known academically as biological anthropology). And thus we may have slightly exaggerated records for "good monsooning" behavior.

However, a bad monsooner is truly not worth having and is illegal in some states. The difference between a good

monsooner and a bad one lies in its size; in the absorptive quality of the coat; in the dog's kinetic potential for reversing the
torque of its skin; and, most critically, in its orientation abilities. Fine working monsoon dogs *always* align their nose-tail
axis parallel to the stem-stern axis of the boat. In the breed
standard, a totally unacceptable fault resulting in immediate
disqualification are dogs orienting transverse to the operational
direction of the boat, known as abaft the beam. This latter position not only does not decrease the amount of water in the boat,
but it also places the dog squarely in front of the person at the
tiller, with highly unsatisfactory results. However, abaft-the-
beam dogs have become more common, making up most of
our pet populations today. The terrible inbreeding has led to
this genetic disease in our purebred dogs. Once they were magnificent animals, useful and functional. Now there is hardly a
dog on the planet that doesn't have a disoriented monsooning
behavior, except the Mexican hairless where it is hard to tell.

When you buy a monsooner it is very, very important to
choose a dog that will match the freeboard of your boat. If
the dog is too tall (or will grow to be too tall)—that is, if its
nose is higher than the gunwale—then the dog won't start
monsooning until you have shipped too much water. Natural
selection will operate to eliminate you and your too-tall dog,
so it is best to register too-tall dogs before they do much harm.
Do keep in mind that too-short dogs have their own problem.
Monsooning below the level of the gunwale just redistributes
the water around inside the boat and, withal, makes it harder

to see where you are going. (See chapter on making your own dog or fixing an imperfect dog.)

As I mentioned earlier, monsooners are ancient dogs and they passed along many traits to modern dogs that have never seen the inside of a boat. Fishermen only rewarded monsooning behavior that was displayed in the presence of people, mostly because it has never been wise to let a dog go fishing alone in a boat. In modern dogs, this genetically programmed oscillatory behavior still needs the physical proximity of a person to elicit the response. My son Tigger's highly bred Chessies will wait, no matter how much they are suffering from waterloggedness, until you admit them into the house, and only there and in the presence of residents do they perform this otherwise highly desirable behavior of expelling scummy swamp water from their coats.

Dogs with the furry above/hairless below configuration sought in monsooners, and with strong oscillatory inclinations, tend to spray dog water on walls and ceiling instead of on the floor where it is easier to clean up. Many wives have adapted to bilge-colored ceilings. What we need to do now is select a dog that has hair on its tummy and nowhere else, perhaps a modified Mexican half-hairless breed, which, regardless of their rotational reciprocations, just dribble. Then all the water would end up on the floor, and none would soak the walls and ceiling and you, except for perhaps your shoes, which may need oiling anyway. While we wait for this new dog to evolve, I suggest you keep a towel rack by the door like we do. Or hire your dogs out to tropical gardens, where they can be useful in recreating tropical rainforest atmospheres.

Monsooners make wonderful pets, a rare quality because good working dogs rarely make good pets. Realize that, at work, these dogs don't do anything unless the water rises in the boat. Since it is unlikely that water will rise in your house, the dog should never really move. What could be a better pet than that? In certain areas of the country that are frequented with hurricanes or flooding, these dogs' instinctual reactions to rising water may inhibit rescue operations. But no dog is perfect all the time and monsooners come highly recommended by those in the know.

BALLAST DOGS

Throughout history, due to the nature of their jobs, the bilgies and monsooners have walked a waterline between life and death. It is not surprising that natural selection has favored the more stable ballast dog.

Like the monsooners, ballast dogs are blue-blooded descendants of the bilge pups. Starting in the depths of shipping, they gradually traded positions, countering the instabilities of the present for the securities of the future. So whenever their vessel started to tip dangerously, they abandoned their downward position, moving to the other (up) side, immediately increasing their chances of survival. This bullish behavior leveraged cargo weight to the highs, countervailing the lows.

Level boats are always a big selective advantage, and people and dogs who make them that way are the real survivors. Over the centuries, the ballast dogs have sub-sub-subdivided into the stalwart bowplunk breeds and the more athletic gyro dogs.

BOWPLUNK DOGS

One of the more famous American ballast dogs is the bow-plunk dog known as the Maine bow dog. This breed was originally recognized by Mr. Barnaby Porter of Damariscotta, Maine. With his kind permission, his breed standard is printed here for the first time, though I'm sure such a fine description has probably been printed in other places for the first time, too.

Bowplunk dog—before and after

Observations on the Maine Bow Dog

by Barnaby Porter

It's time the Maine coon cat was put in its place. It has been highly overrated as a breed all these years, and I'm not so sure anyone has a true and accurate idea of just what makes a coon cat a coon cat anyhow. It's an appellation that has come to have about as much meaning as "colonial farmhouse." Rather common-looking balls of fluff are what they are.

Of much more convincing pedigree is a hardy and noble breed of dog, heretofore not made much of because of its humble beginnings and conspicuous absence from the show ring. This is the magnificent Maine bow dog, his name deriving from his deeply ingrained habit of standing, proud and brave, on the bow of his master's boat as it plies the lively waters along the Maine coast.

There is nothing quite so moving as the sight of such a dog holding his station, ears flying and a big smile on his face, as his sturdy vessel bounds over the sparking whitecaps, his profile emblazoned on the horizon.

The points of conformation in the bow dog breed are far from strict. The dog's size, color and general appearance have nothing to do with it. Even pom-pom tails are allowed. Good claws are the only mandatory physical attribute. It's mostly a matter of character and carriage. The animal must have superb footing and balance, and most important, he must display the eagerness and bravery of the true bow dog. A passion for boats and the water is essential, for the dog must be willing and able to maintain the classic stance, chin up and chest out, in even gale force winds.

Individual bow dogs may vary greatly in style, but their dedication to duty must be unquestionable. One I know, named Wontese, who looks something like a springer spaniel, is such a glutton for cold and punishing duty that his uncontrolled but enthusiastic chattering has become legendary. Another, named Duke, wears a sou'wester. Remarkable, these dogs.

Being in the working dog class, bow dogs are permitted the occasional slipup to be expected in the real world conditions under which they must perform. Mine, an almost flawless specimen, was most embarrassed one day when he broke stance for a brief moment to take a flea break. There was a blustery chop in the sea, and in a flash, he slipped ingloriously over the side, his gleaming claws raking the bow as he disappeared from sight. A valuable dog like that, I had to come around and fish him out of the waves. I hoisted his drenched bulk back aboard, and without so much as a thought about shaking off, he leaped up forward to where he belonged, brave and proud, ears flying.

That's a Maine bow dog if I've ever seen one. It made me proud to be his master.

Mr. Porter obviously knows his dogs, and he does a good job of reporting on the courage and nobility of this breed, which stands in the bows of fishing boats and looks good no matter what—even though there is great variability in the way they look. (This is lucky, however, because there is a similar variability in the looks of Maine fishing boats and even greater variability in the looks of Maine fishermen. Matching bow dog to boat should not be the problem it is with the baildales.) Mr. Porter seems unaware that his dog belongs to a functional breed classically known as the ballast dog, and though he does not realize that the breed is highly functional, he misses the connection between the dog's function and its "conspicuous absence from the show ring," since it is not registered with any kennel club in the world, so far as I know.

The purpose of a ballast dog standing in the bow (the front, or pointy end of the boat) is to hold it down in the water while you paddle or steer from the stern. (The reason it is called the stern is because it is a very serious part of the boat, being where you hang the outboard motor, and steer from.) Trolling (named after the character who fished under bridges when you were a little kid) also takes place in the stern. Really good bow dogs have an innate sense of "trim." As the speed of the boat increases, the dog leans farther and farther forward, keeping the boat "trimmed," or relatively even in the water.

Mr. Porter was on the right track when he listed the problem areas in Maine bow dogs. He correctly points out that they should be agile, as well as able to concentrate for long periods of time and avoid fleeting distractions. This means a good Maine bow dog really ought not fall overboard. Natural selection would have taken care of this problem years ago, if only fishermen would just keep going and tend to business instead of forgiving a fallen dog. But the dog is half of a closely-bonded team, and that attachment is rarely ruptured just because one member of the party made a mistake. To be honest, if one does rescue a fallen dog, at least one should have the courtesy of registering it with the kennel club.

Very few fishermen have the sheer Darwinian courage not to turn back in an attempt to rescue a fallen bow wow, and this prevailing softheartedness has been a large factor in the dog's morphology: a successful bow dog has a hefty scruff. Scruffs[17] were an early adaptation in this breed, developed even before the perfection of bowplunk behavior. And it's easy to see why. When a stabilizing bowplunk dog goes overboard in heavy seas, the danger of capsizing is doubly great: leaning over the side and grabbing a struggling dog by the scruff of its neck can be a selective disadvantage for both symbionts.

However, scruffs do have a disagreeable side effect when combined with monsooning behavior. Monsooning is, for the Maine bow dog, vestigio-functionless (technically speaking). After the dog's unplanned baptism and resurrection (and only in the immediate proximity of a human), its preprogrammed, metronomic monsooning behavior is unleashed. And, of

---

[17]   The name of the famous British dog show is adapted from this organ.

course, because no one has ever thought to breed good monsooners (see page 57) with good bow dogs (see Mr. Porter's description), this syncopated shiver and splatter is never displayed in the bowplunk position (forward in the bow), but rather in the stem (or middle) of the boat where the central axis of the dog is abaft the beam and upwind. Mr. Porter's dog is the only one I have ever heard of that skipped what he calls shaking off and went right back to his post. But the mere fact that he mentioned it suggests that he might be fibulating.

In the absence of a monsooner × bow dog cross-breed, training a substitute behavior in your bow dog is nearly impossible. And, of course, trimming the scruff is highly unethical (as well as dangerous) and in some states illegal. Reward and punishment models are tough to effect: many times I have stood in the athwart position with a large stick (two-by-four), ready to demonstrate disapproval, only to be thrown off by vigorous monsoon.

The relationship between dog and man—a team inseparable through thick and thin—man's best friend—all of that is hogwash—did you ever see a dog go back and rescue a fisherman who has fallen overboard? The dog is simply doing what it was selected to do.

I have mixed feelings about bowplunks as pets. Their ancestries make them loyal companions, but a little bit of the "one-man dog" type, thus they don't make very good family dogs. My main complaint is this: in a boat they know exactly where to go, but how those instincts get expressed in a house is problematic and they tend to wander and go everywhere.

GYRO DOGS

The gyro dog was derived during ancient fishing days, when boats were really tippy. Back then, the boat builders' union agreed (this time with each other) to make all boats that would and could last forever—unless they sank. Leaks might have done the trick, but monsooners took care of minor leaks. Starting in the Preamblelithic Age in Indiana, shipbuilders went to tippy canoes. Marine architects everywhere began almost immediately designing in instability as a kind of planned obsolescence.[18] Encouraged by their guild, producers and designers thereby kept production at a maximum while still crafting seemingly good-quality boats.

Lost in the mist nets of antiquity is a story of how fishermen came up with the idea of separate but equally weighted dogs to counterbalance their tippy bateaux. The gyro dog is my favorite, using the same gimbalic principle of the gyro compass, with an organic difference. The dog simply goes to the opposite side of the boat from the fisherman. This counterbalances the fishing activities.

Not lost in the mists of antiquity is the authentication of Greek gyro dogs as the first examples of purebred, function-specific ballast dogs. Marco Polo, returning from China to the Mediterranean world, is said to have brought with him the ancestors of these dogs—bilge pups, of course—along

---

[18] My fishing buddy Stan says this was maybe the only time in economic history where union and management worked to mutual benefit.

with other curiosities like spaghetti. The Greeks developed the best gyros.

Greek fisherman found that around lunchtime these bilges had a tendency to go to the opposite side of the boat from the fisherman. This was natural to gyros, given their origins as the world's first junk food. As the fisherman chased the dogs around the boat, the boat stayed level. Eureka! Several dialogues later, the next logical question arose: how could you get the boat to stay level during the non-pre-lunch periods?

The Greeks developed two solutions to the tippy problem, both of which are still used. The first solution was simply to lunch all the time. (Stan's a champion at this, dragging out the pre-breakfast period, during which our boat is always level because nobody is in it for most of the morning, and so no fishing is going on, and subsequently, he's trying to find where he stowed the ingredients for lunch, which worries me as well as the dog.)

The second solution was to wear a mask on the back of the head with a fierce, hungry-looking face on it. It was a matter of simple Skinnerian conditioning to elicit the dog's "180-degrees-away" motion in reaction to the mask. Primary conditioning was accomplished with the fisherman facing the dog, using his own face to show how hungry he was. Once the dog was conditioned to move away from this expression, the fisherman wore the hungry face on the back of his head, thus maintaining the boat's delicate balance at all times. The resulting breed was the Greek gyro. Once per-fected, many of these gyros became real heroes.[19]

Gyro dog—gyroing

In tippy fishing boats, balance is everything. With a good fighting bluefish skiffing about, now on this side, now on that, a good gyro dog will just about run himself to death trying to stay opposite the fisherman. If you use these dogs, remember that it is important to keep the boat free of treble hooks and other debris. Not only are sharp, pointy little things hazardous for the dog, but if the dog has to jump over them, his counter-balancing weight appears and disappears from the surface of the boat, causing a dangerous oscillation (technically known as a gyration). A really top-notch gyro will keep one foot on the deck of the boat at all times, correcting any oscillations created by herself or the fisherman.

---

[19] I should point out that one school of anthropology credits the gyros to the Sub-Sandwich Islanders. See "anthropologists agree" footnote, page 17.

Before you invest in a gyro, take it out for a test-fish—or at least watch how it reacts to your hungry face. Stanley had this one dog he named Hoagie. Nice dog, but totally unsuitable for fishing. This dog was afraid of nothing—which, as you may guess, is a fault in this breed; good gyros are innately afraid of being eaten. But Hoagie actually looked forward to breakfast. He did his share of the work by doing the dishes every morning, and sometimes he gave them another swipe when we got back in the evening. He was very good at getting the little lumps off the bottom of the frying pan. Next thing, though, Stanley got the dog interested in fishing. Disaster. Right in the middle of the excitement, the darn dog would come over to see if you were catching a keeper for supper.

A good gyro dog makes a perfect pet. With their built-in instinct to always go away from people, especially at meal time, the dog is always on the other side of the house and you never see them—no more perfect dog than that.

Chapter 8

Already-Bailed-Dales

The gillie dogs that really go overboard are the already-bailed-dales, including the stringer spaniels, with a notable sub-species, the hatch-match spaniels. The noblest of the gillie dogs, for my money, are the floating mat dogs, along with their subspecies, which are too numerous to mention here.

FLOATING MAT DOGS

Floating mat dogs are the elite among fishing dogs. They are the cleverest, the most fun to work with, and they make the best house dogs I know. They don't chase cats or cars. They don't have that in-and-out-all-the-time behavior. For the most part, you can put a floating mat dog anywhere and it is no more trouble than the average scatter rug. Once in a while it's good to vacuum-clean them.

Out in the field, they assist in a variety of ways. Since, like all dogs, they are waterproof, and fur is a good insulator, they can be draped over minnow pails when the sun is hot or over lunch bags on rainy days. (In lunch bag situations, it's wise to keep the head end of the dog away from the soft parts of the lunch.) The first fishing dog I ever had was a floating mat dog.

Years ago, shortly before our trial separation, Stan and I began going to Ontario to fish. We usually went every fall, just before school opened, to get our heads straight before we had to go back to work. Our quarry was northern pike. For those of you who are just interested in dogs and don't know much about fishing, you have to understand that fall fishing for pike consists mostly of casting into weeds, grasses, lily pads, and snags. This was the first method I'd learned, and Stan taught it to me. It is the standard method of catching August "hammer-handle" pike.

One year we changed our routine slightly, so that as soon as school was over in the spring, we headed north. This got our heads straighter earlier, and we figured we could still go again in August. But the real reason for the May foray was to catch big pike. You catch big pike just after ice-out. Spring fishing for humongous pike is in the flats or where they cruise along rocky shores or windswept points, or on the edge of the ice, or maybe in deep holes or at the mouths of little streams. You fish anywhere except under weeds, grasses, and lily pads because there are no weeds, grasses, and lily pads in the spring. That's because weeds, grasses, and lily pads haven't grown up yet. That's because the water isn't warm enough for weeds, grasses, and lily pads yet, and because the ice hasn't uncovered the weeds, grasses, and lily pads yet, and for a thousand other reasons, including that Mother Nature doesn't like weeds, grasses, and lily pads in the spring.

Our problem was Stan, bless his heart. Talk about trying to teach an old dog a new trick. (In fact, I've learned a lot about training dogs from watching Stan.) When you're fishing for pike with Stan, you're casting to weeds, grasses, or lily pads. That's the way to fish for pike, according to Stan. He's dogmatic about this. This is the way we did it on the Mattagami and the Kapuskasing Rivers. That is the way we always caught pike and so there is no other way.

"Stan," I said one day, "let's troll a rocky windswept point."

He looked at me as if I were stupid. "You can't find weeds on a rocky windswept point," he said, patiently.

But off we went, scraping the bottom of the boat, and the propeller, in shallows that would have pike grass in two months. The lone lily pad was still shivering so hard it would scare the pike. But there was no arguing with Stan, and we floated around in the little bays like Sir John Franklin looking for the Northwest Passage.

That summer was when we tried the trial separation, and our therapist talked us into getting a dog in order to give our relationship more stability. She thought if we could focus on someone else's needs rather than being selfishly anchored over invisible weed beds, it might ease the tension.

So I did the research, Stan chipped in his half, as usual, if I did all the work, and by the next year's ice-out, we had this amazing dog—our first floating mat dog. We were so happy. Not only did he give us something to take care of besides ourselves, but we could use him in the spring to simulate the floating mats of weeds that we needed to cast to.

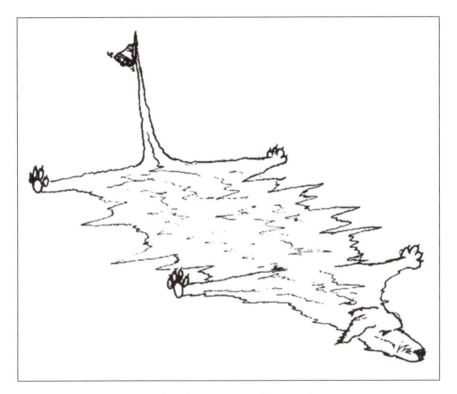

The perfect floating mat dog, Mathew.

Stan called the pup Mat, which I thought was pretty unimaginative. I bet half the dogs in the Floating Mat Dog

Association are named Mat: Doormat, Welcome Mat, Automat, and Matilda. (Other people with floating mat dogs name them after some specific kind of floating vegetation like Lily Pad, or Hyacinth, and once in a while you'll get a Sargasso, or just plain Scum. One of my cleverer colleagues, a marine ecologist, named her mat dog Phydeauxplankton, or Phydeaux for short.) When I mentioned the lack of imagination issue to Stan in a nice way, he said the name was short for Matthew and he always wanted a dog named Matthew. That confused me because if he wanted a dog named Matthew, why would he call him Mat? Why not do the yuppie bit and call him Thew? It just didn't make sense, but since I was trying to make this relationship work, I let it go and we both began using the affectionate form, "Matty."

Floating Mat Dog Evolution

The nearest I can figure the first mat dog for fishing probably happened in Florida in the late-nineteenth century. The original stock was bilge pups of the monsoon strain, which came ashore when some Spanish galleon sank. For a little while, the conquistadors used the dogs as saddle blankets for their ponies, but they ended up like most horse products—strewn around the yard, unnoticed for years.

Now, in Florida there has been a long tradition of cleaning the yard by throwing everything into the lake. Some fishermen (mowing the lawn) must have chucked one of those old bilge pup remnants into the pond, where it floated. Fish swam under the shadow, using it the same way they use overhanging rocks or weeds.

Fish like shady places. Fish stuck in the middle of a pond would have as much trouble with ozone holes as we do. Fish in bright light are seen more easily by birds and become vulnerable to predation. Little fish experiencing this problem hide in shadows and big fish trying to eat little fish hide in the same shadows, while male fish looking for lovers hide in the shadows because that is where female fish will be finding food to make eggs. Many of life's strategies take place in the shadows. This is why you cast to lily pads and logs. It is well known that fish don't like bright lights, but it is not so well known that in most ponds there is not enough shade for everybody. Shade is an "ecological limiting factor," which means that there might not be enough shade for all those fish that require shade. And it is this situation that the fisherman and his floating mat dog exploit.

A group of fishermen, known affectionately to each other as Crackers, had the same problem. These Saltines, who fished offshore, fathomed that out in the Atlantic Ocean there is the same amount of shade as in the middle of the Sahara Desert. Realizing that you can't find fish in the middle of the Sahara, they searched for shade and found it under the giant manta rays. Under these slowly gliding tarpaulins, all the fish in the world are stacked up, each trying to get a little drift of shadow.

The Saltines are pretty smart cookies, so they thought they would get a manta mimic. One of them (a fisherman on temporary lawn-mowing duty) had a dog that looked like a tangle of lily pads, which his wife used to cover a bare spot in the lawn. If he could get it to act like a bunch of lily pads in a backwater, his fishing future would be assured.

Fishing a floating mat

Kazaam! Those lily pad/weed mimics were all over the backyards of Florida: dogs with lots of stringy hair with things growing in it. Flat, motionless dogs with quiet but uplifting personalities. Dogs that had spent generations collecting shade, waiting for the time to give some back. Here were dogs fore-shadowing a revolution in evolution: preadapted slough-hole yard dogs became floating mat dogs—a useful and valuable breed. This was evolution without change, something every conservationist dreams of.

The floating mat dogs instantly achieved behavioral perfection. They still exhibit all the same behaviors while floating in a bayou, pond, or lake that their ancestors did on a sultry afternoon when the burglars arrived. These may not be the kind of dogs that jump into pickup trucks (or even jump out of one), but when you get to the lake and float one, it is a pure thrill to watch it in inaction.

Training and Fishing Your Mat Dog

Because I'm a biologist, I got to raise and train Matty over that first winter. Training is not hard, because basically the floating mat dog will just float on the water wherever you leave it. Find a fishing area in at least four to six feet of water and gently slip the mat dog over the side, allowing its hair to fully spread out over the water. The dog's legs should extend along with the hair and be held in a quarterly pattern.

That's it. You can increase your mat dog's value by training it to take an active interest in the sport so that it watches underneath itself and gently raises its tail when a legal-sized fish is present. A bell on its tail helps to rouse a drowsy fisherman.

Matty got the hang of his job right off and started to embellish. He would mimic all kinds of vegetation. His best was eel grass: the first time I saw his eel grass I thought he was just cold, but what he was doing was raising his hair above the water and letting it bend slightly in the wind. What artistry! It looked so natural, the way the hair would tip and then shake slightly just as though a little breeze had come along. One morning I could have sworn I saw a floating basket with a little Moses, but it was just Matthew, trying out another image.

Longhaired mat dogs can't swim very well because their spread-out legs get tangled in the tresses. Thus, when the wind is blowing (not a problem in the early morning before breakfast) or currents are brisk, Stan and I recommend anchoring the dog by its collar. If there is too much wind or current, then a belt around the dog's waist allows it to drift headfirst, downwind or down-current. The anchor rope should be at least three times the depth of the water, as a rope that is too short will cause the dog's head to be pulled below the surface, causing an unnecessary commotion and scaring the fish.

The secret is to get the drift right. Gently pitch a dog out to a strategic location, and you'll have the time of your life. Mud and other debris naturally tangled in the dog's coat are an advantage, making him appear more authentic. Insects buzzing around a mat dog are usually plentiful, probably because the moisture balance in the hair is conducive to the growth and reproduction of pesky six-leggers. Their regular appearance at the periphery of the working mat dog is an aid in attracting the feeding fish. There is no "matching the hatch" problem with a well-unkempt floating mat dog.

Could fool a bird

Casting to a floating dog mat should be done carefully. You have to cast over the dog, letting the lure drift off slightly with the wind. This way the retrieve won't snag the dog. It is important not to snag especially young dogs because you can easily sour them on fishing.

They begin to flinch as you cast to them, scaring the fish below. Spinner baits work well but buzz baits tickle, forcing the dog into compulsive scratching, which, again, scares the fish.

At noon, the shadow is directly below the dog, but it varies with time of day and season, and you will have to adjust your casting. Try to cast to the shadow side of the dog, west in the morning and east in the afternoon if you're in the northern

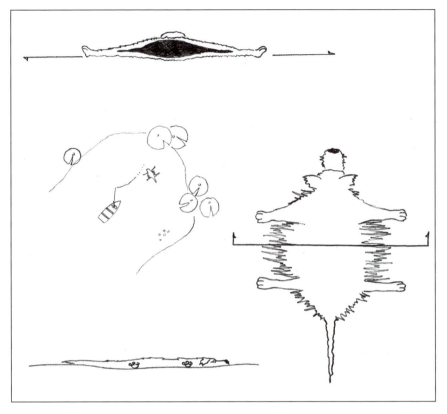

Floating mat dog—conformation standards

hemisphere. This keeps your hook closer to the fish. Be aware of the wind, because it can affect your cast. You need to adjust your boat to the wind and to the shadow angle, always mindful of the hook/dog relationship.

Before you float a mat dog, remove all the shiny metal tags from its collar. Many top-level toothy piscivorous fish (pike and muskies are good examples) can't tell the difference between a rabies tag and a silver spoon. I once had a pike strike savagely at a dog tag and try to swim off with my dog. This is another good way to sour a dog.

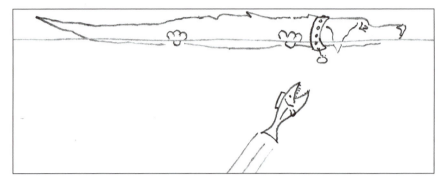

Floating mat—fishing no-no

When I'm fishing pike, pickerel, or muskies, I prefer female mat dogs. Their profiles in the water are smoother and nothing hangs down to attract snacking fish. Older male dogs can get nervous in muskie country and that nervousness gets passed on to the fishermen, making the cast rate go way up. Neutering the dog sometimes solves a couple of problems.

So far there are no laws about how many mat dogs you can use, but the time surely will come. Some fishermen attach a small flag to the dog's tail so it looks like a tip-up for ice fishing. While this is certainly an aid when you are using ten or more dogs, I feel this practice may lead to laws that equate the dogs to mechanical devices, and their use will be restricted to six or seven dogs at any one time. Legislation has already been drafted in England to prevent the floating of many dogs, although mat dogs are popular there. The British seem to prefer dogs that don't do anything and these dogs are naturals at that. Also, you can fish in the noonday sun, which is good for both mat dogs and Englishmen.

Floating mat—working versatility

Choosing a Mat Dog

I like brown mat dogs with some water-lily yellow streaking. Recently, several people have reported good luck with black dogs. Green would be best, but my geneticist friends say green is impossible to select for in a dog. The rare white mat dog can be dyed green, but this is expensive, as not many grooming parlors carry green in sizes larger than a toy poodle.[20]

Conformation and breed standard is very important in floating mat dogs. Seen from above, the good ones have an almost

---

[20] Some Chessies are supposed to be a "dead grass" color, and that is not very different from "peat bog." At least the Chessies my son has are very close to that color, especially when they are lying on the dining room rug. It is one of those mysteries of evolution, where the background of an animal's preferred habitat begins to look like the animal. In just a few short years, all our rugs have taken on a dead grass color.

perfectly round appearance when floating on a pond. From a side view, however, they are almost flat. This flatness gives added surface area and, therefore shadow, and also means they pack well. Some fishermen just roll them up and store them in PVC pipes on the roof of the van.

As for old Matthew, disaster eventually struck our faithful first mat dog. I really can't blame it all on Stan. Stan hadn't noticed that I'd put Matty in the van, and he piled all the gear on him. I think it was all those plastic milk crates full of frying pans and other kitchen paraphernalia that did him in. So help me, we never gave it a thought until we were unloading at the float plane. When we discovered Matty on the bed of the van, we suspected the worst, but given the true-to-breed nature and conformation of the dog, it was difficult to tell how bad it was. We decided to give him the benefit of the doubt and fished him. He seemed to do pretty well for a couple of days before it became clear that his soul was in a different place. This was no fluke. He was dead. It is now many years later and we have a kennel full of floating mats, but we always remember that Matthew came first. He was a true fisher among dogs.

Recently Stanley has been cheating a bit, doing a little fishing on the side with this other guy Randy MacDonald. I pretend I don't know. But Randy is one of these experimenters and started breeding his own mat dogs and, of course, like many amateurs, the "bigger is better" syndrome looms large. So finally he has a kennel full of really—I mean really—big dogs and needs to sell some off. There you got it—signs and ads for Randy MacDonald's big mats. My God, you have to have a flatbed truck to get one home. I swear you don't even need a boat. Randy has a bracket that slides over the dog's tail for mounting the outboard right on the dog. Next thing, he'll have a potted palm tree in the center and a couple of lawn chairs for he and Stan.

Off-Season Care and Maintenance of a Big Mat

Floating mat dogs are tough to exercise in the off-season. I tried leaving one in a nearby pond while I went to work, but an early freeze-up discouraged me from doing that again. Many are too big for the bathtub, and my wife objects to using the swimming pool if they are shedding. But keeping your dog in all winter and letting it lie in front of the fireplace with your fly rod hanging over the mantel looks great, although both the rod and the dog will dry out.

Floating Mats as Pets

As pets, their inability to walk leads to those "in the way" hazards. The result is putting them out of the way, and guess what—they get forgotten. They go unnoticed and perhaps even neglected. The worst is that if the females come into heat in some out-of-the-way-place, they can be bred by some slimy intruder and you might not know it for nine weeks. Now for the first time, we are faced with the mongrel fishing dog, which instead of being a good-looking mat looks more like a rag rug.

Some people have tried showing floating mats. Field trials are okay, but at your standard dog show, getting them around the ring is a problem. People have tried dragging them around on trolleys. But that means they have to change the rules and allow all the dogs that can't walk to participate in Special Dog Shows.

FLOUNDERHOUNDERS

Imperfection is what evolution is all about, and that's as true for dogs as it is for fishing buddies. But, since the beginning of time, breeders have capitalized on imperfection. If that weren't the case, we wouldn't have half the dogs we do today.

Breeders of purebred dogs are people who preserve nature's major anomalies. How else could they have turned the dog morphologically into the most varied species in the world? When man came along, the natural world was full. There was a species in every niche. Nothing more could happen. But dog breeders discovered a way to put some life into modern evolution: adaptation is passé; maladaptation is au courant. Strive not for perfection of form, but take tiny maladaptive characteristics and perfect them. For example, clever breeders have perfected the snore. Breeds like the Boston terrier and English bulldog may not be able to do anything else well, but they can snore better than any creature on earth. Hungarian breeders have perfected the coats on their dogs so nothing can get through them except some specialized smells. The puli and the komondor have such perfect coats that you can't even get a snarl out of them.

The other thing that breeders are really good at thinking up purposes for genetic anomalies they've perfected. After all, the dog should behave the way it looks. If the wolf could have only known what it was coming to. . . .

Just when you think breeders have separated all the different conformations, shapes, sizes, and colors into separate breeds, along comes the flounderhounder. The flounderhounder is the most striking of all the dog anomalies.

This is not my favorite breed of dog, and I don't recommend them as working dogs or even as pets. But since I'm trying to be complete and give the reader the whole picture of the dog world, I feel obligated to include the flounderhounder.

Some time ago, a variety of dogs was found in Louisiana that were so lazy they must have lain on their self-same side

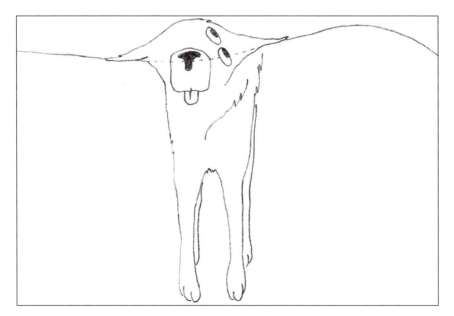

The flounderhounder

throughout evolutionary history. One eye, usually the left, has migrated to the right side of the head, so the dog has two eyes on that side. The migration of the eye wasn't noticed for a long time, which is understandable under the circumstances.

In the early evolutionary period of the eye (the paleolidics), the dog's left eye was in the down position, looking directly into the lawn. Because it was geologically a very damp period, the dog often kept the eye shut tightly. Of course, even a tight eyelid can still leak. Thus natural selection favored those dogs whose eyelids grew permanently shut, giving the dog a leak-less disposition, and preventing any foreign substances whatsoever from infecting the eyeball.

By keeping such a tight lid on, the down eye couldn't see. But this wasn't really a selective disadvantage because it couldn't see very far into the lawn anyway.[21] Another reason these dogs couldn't see well was that they were mostly asleep.[22]

Throughout the mesolidic eye-evolution process, the vestigial eye went looking for something to do. Thus it migrated through the head. This developmental process, like all evolutionary advancements, had to be done very slowly. This was not because there were obstacles to the migration, but rather because it didn't know where to go. For a long period

---

[21] The eyes of several other dog breeds are also vestigial: for example, the breeds with the hanging gardens of Babylon covering their faces, so that nothing including light is allowed to get through to the dog.

[22] Sleep is an energy-saving behavior perfected by dogs. Scientists have not found any other species that conserves as much energy as the domestic dog. Conservationists have nominated the dog for a sustainable-energy award.

of time, while the eye was in the middle of the head (halfway between where it was in ancestral times and where it ended up in descendent times[23]), nobody noticed that the dog didn't have an eye on the down side.

Next came the neolidic period of the flounderhounder's development, popularly known as the Cajun Surprise. One day, a bayou buster went to feed the dog and the dog was looking at him with two eyes. As always, the dog looked pleased with himself and wagged his tail.

Zappo! The guy becomes an instant expert dog breeder on the basis of this one dog with both eyes on the same side. This is not unusual for dog breeders. They discover that there is something different about their dog and *pesto!* They start another breed. Technically they are giving the dog "a sporting chance." Why waste time breeding the best to the best in some slow evolutionary fashion when you could put a little English on it? Besides, breeding the best to the best in dogs means breeding the best looking ones, and for flounderhounders, the best looking ones had both eyes on the same side of the head.

Once this one-sided looking behavior was discovered, it was thought that the dog might be pre-adapted to specialized work. Breeders first tried fishing the dog for flounder (if it

---

[23] Descendent may be a confusing term because the eye was moving up or ascending. Ascendant might be a better word since this is an evolutionary advancement: the ancestral form and the ascendant form. Humans are the only real descendants because they came down out of the trees. Technically, domestication cannot be either an ascent or descent because it is an unnatural selection—especially where the dog is concerned.

Fishing a flounderhounder

looked like one, it should act like one). This is the single instance in the dog world where function followed looks.

Flounderhounders tend to be flatter than mat dogs, because people in Louisiana tend to mow their lawns. Therefore, the dogs have very little lung capacity and tend to sink. Breeders theorized if they had small lungs it was an adaptation to not needing air, just like the bulldog people selected for nose plugs in their dogs because they only needed air for snoring. Next, since the dog sinks to the bottom of the lake, they thought it was adapted to lying on the bottom pretending to be a rock pile or a reproductively active flounder.

Some saw this as an alternative to the floating mat dog. Instead of spreading the shadow from the top of the water (as a floating mat does), where the shadow gets diffused by light leaking from the sides, the flounderhounder, lying directly on the bottom, has the best quality shadow of any of the already-bailed-dales. I don't find this particularly useful, actually, because even though the shadow is superbly dark, the dog doesn't cast enough of it. The total volume of shadow can be calculated by multiplying the surface area of dog by the depth of the water under the dog. Therefore, a three-foot diameter (93 cm) mat dog in four feet (113.5 cm) of water gives 28.3 cubic feet (6793 cubic cm) of shade. The same sized flounderhounder settling to the bottom would give you seven square feet (and zero cubic feet) of shade. And why would you want a dog with seven square feet?

The breed's lack of lung capacity is actually an adaptation to long periods of dormancy. As a front dormancy, flounderhounders make nice welcome mats, wagging their tails but not leaping up to paw or sniff. They are easy to store in the off-season, and many people use flounderhounders as scatter rugs. But don't try to fish one. No matter what the breeders tell you, they *do* need air. The best you can do is use them in the intertidal flat, but only when the tide is out. And by the way—hint, hint—when the tide is out, the fishing isn't great. My advice is: just leave the breed with the show people. Let them add it to their growing collection of unusual dogs. Mixed matings are often disastrous. Imagine an accident between a flounderhounder crossed with a beagle.

You get three eyes on one side of the dog's head all wound up together and just one eye on the other side looking lonely. Poor dog couldn't tell which eye it was looking out and when.

Flounderhounders as Pets

Now that I think on it, they might make good watch dogs with the two eyes on top and no chance of curling up and missing something. Then again, they really shouldn't bark because when they're working, they would fill up with water.

LOG DOGS

Another type of already-bailed-dale is the log dog. These floaters are a remarkable example of the evolutionary principle of convergence: coming from a completely different ancestral strain (the punting dogs), log dogs now perform a similar task for the fisherman as the floating mat dogs do.

Log dogs were developed by a few smart hunters (they are too few to list their names here). They are therefore an illustration of the evolutionary principle of taking something good and making it much more useful; for example, taking a hunting dog and making it into a fishing dog. The first log dogs were short-legged Chesapeake Bay retrievers (market hunting dogs). This local variety was developed in the early 1800s in the Upper Bay Area, where punt gunners bred and trained their dogs to swim alongside their boats and not get in and out all the time.

Major Digression: Imagining Duck Hunting in the nineteenth Century and At Other Times.

Now, many of us have trouble imagining just what the nineteenth century was like. Foraging for wild game was much more important then, simply because the supermarket had not been invented yet. Wild things cluttered the landscape, darkened the sun, and clogged the rivers. People tried to solve both problems by eating them all, but they had to double their own population to accomplish this task. Hunters specialized in eliminating certain kinds of wildlife; the commercial punt gunners were really challenged by the terrific numbers of ducks and waterfowl that lived in or migrated through the Chesapeake Bay.

Hunters were better in the nineteenth century. They could get all the game and sometimes, as in the case of the passenger pigeon, they did. Dogs were better, too. Today, bird-dog owners brag that their dogs can do "doubles," and if Curly can do triples, he gets written up in a national magazine. In the nineteenth century, a dog might bring in three hundred ducks a day for a punt gunner. That's about one duck every two and a half minutes.

Now imagine a typical punt hunter's day. At around half past five in the afternoon, he shoots the 280th duck. He has to "mark" each bird for the dog, like we do today; "Meat [dog's name], ober dhare Meat," he says, pointing to the 280th duck of the day. Mercy. The guy would be popping throat lozenges like a drug addict and he'd have punt gunner's finger, worn out from pointing. If Meat was anything like my son's Chessies, the guy would also have a frozen finger, because the dog has to see the actual finger in order to get the correct general direction. There is no hiding the finger in a glove for these highly trained, intelligent dogs. As every cognitive psychologist knows, the dog needs to see the real finger. One Hungarian study says that really long fingers (the longer the better) work best for giving the dog the correct direction.

For the 280th time, Meat leaps out of the boat,[24] giving it a little thrust backward as he accelerates forward. Therefore, each time Meat leaps out of the boat, he has to swim farther and farther to the ducks because the boat would be getting farther and farther away.

---

[24] Again, if Meat is anything like my son's dogs, he would be very discerning about where he jumps over the side of the boat. Tigger's Chessies run around at the gunwales for about ten minutes looking for the exact right spot. We had to switch to padded fiberglass boats because the ticky-tucky of their little nails on the aluminum made an unpleasant sound on a wet, raw duck-hunting day. Often, we wore earmuffs even on warm and delightful days.

Now the worst part—Meat has to get back into the boat. The process is defined as "clambering in." If I may extrapolate from my son's dogs, I'd guess Meat could turn that boat's sides to hamburger in just 280 ducks. Have you ever seen a dog clamber into a boat? It's just too incredible. Somebody should make a movie! My son's old Chessie, Scoter, had to be the all-time champion at clambering. Placing her forefeet on the gunwale, she would begin a series of cranking motions with her left hind foot. Against the side of an aluminum boat, it sounded melodic and eerie, increasing in tempo until it brought to mind the Andrew Sisters singing eight-to-the-bar.[25]

Each rotation of the leg and foot would gain her a millimeter in the up-and-in direction. The leg would now be going at the speed of light, but, unlike the arm of an old record player that follows the groove, this armature creates its own grooves in the side of the boat.

Faster and faster, the leg dug for bauxite. After several minutes, she would get her head over the gunwale. The second movement involved a tympanic percussion solo as she positioned her head under the seat. Initially this "head

---

[25] We keep Scoter in shape in the off-season by turning her on her back and scratching that magic spot on her tummy, triggering the phantom-scratching reflex. First one side, then the other. A couple of isometric minutes a day is all that's needed to keep her ready for boat clambering.

tuck under seat" motion would be accomplished with a harmonized drumming of the top of her head on the bottom of the seat. Then came the Anne Boleyn movement: with her head . . . tucked . . . underneath the seat . . . she walked . . . her head along . . . leveraging with her neck and bringing her body up horizontal to the plane of the water.

Once Scoter got her head firmly lodged under the seat, both hind feet could work in harmony, though she often jazzed it up with syncopation. The final movement started with an arpeggio of elbow, which breached the gunwale.[26]

With a final drumming roll, the dog was in. A lot of sea water came in, too. This drained immediately into the bilge where it began to separate into layers. The heavy water sank to the bottom while the finer grades of Chesapeake oils sat delicately on top. In the early stages of separation, one got quite colorful little rainbow effects.

But Scoter is a direct descendant of the bilgies (yes, Chessies have that distinction[27]), and duty called her. There was water in the boat, which instinct demanded she must expel. She must, inevitably, monsoon. She

---

[26]   The gunwale ("gun wall") is the top side of the boat where the cannon was installed; it was not only instrumental in letting the cannonball out, but to this day it remains important for not letting the water in.

[27]   Chesapeake Bay retrievers were bilge pups as late as the nineteenth century; legend has it that a breeding pair were washed out from the bilge of a shipwreck off the coast of Maryland in 1807.

often stood, not in the fore-and-aft-the-beam position, but rather in the straddle-the-thwart position, while monsooning. Now the rainbows were really gorgeous. She is not a lazy dog and would continue this health-giving behavior until all the water was gone, no matter how long it took. I say health-giving because my cigar often went out with the first monsoon and was usually unrelightable.

I'm not quite sure what happened next because I regularly used the intermission to clean my glasses. But I think this was when she presented the bouquet of duck to Tigger. The performance over, we'd get busy again, cleaning the salt spray off our guns so they wouldn't pit and making the usual duct tape repairs on the seat cushions. Now came the part of the performance that I lived for.

Tigger would raise his frozen finger toward the open sea, and say, "Fetch." Yes, Scoter could do doubles. But she always, after numerous circumlocutions, left the boat from the same spot. I don't know if it was just instinct or whether Tigger taught her this way. Whatever, she usually forgot where that special place was, and she searched rapidly for it, disturbing the little layerings of water, which again made little rainbows of protest as they figured out their layer patterning once more.

It will be pretty obvious to the reader that the early punt gunner couldn't have Meat get in and out of the boat three hundred times a day. Based on our experience with Scoter, in three hundred retrieves Meat could wear out a boat a day.

No. The dog had to stay in the water, out with the decoys if possible. If it could learn to anticipate the shooting and be there, the dog only had to swim one way (back to the boat) after the duck was shot.

BALTIMORE DUCK HEADED LOGDOG DOGS (BDHLD)

As I said many times, you can't stop evolution. Some of these beside-the-punt dogs have evolved into the Baltimore duck heads.

It ain't what it seems.

The BDHLD dogs shouldn't be in this book because they aren't strictly fishing dogs but rather hunting dogs—a duck hunting dog to be exact. But they are the ancestor to the log dogs and therefore come into the picture. At its most effective, this in-water retriever had a head that stuck out of the water (this is important for several reasons), and it (the head) looked kinda like a duck.

Some dogs, mostly Chesapeake Bay retrievers, had really ducky heads and floated low in the water with only their head showing. This resulted in an almost-perfect duck mimic, so they could be used as decoys as well as retrievers. Properly trained, such dogs were actually better than wooden decoys: their moving around, sniffing noses, and generally taking an interest in each other made for realistic, ducky behavior.

It still ain't what it seems.

Using wooden decoys is a troublesome affair.

Problem: Before you start off on a duck hunt, you have to find the decoys—they got moved around since last fall to some place you don't know.

Solution: With BDHLD dogs, you just call them and tell them to go get in the car.

Problem: When you get to the hunting site, the blind is still there, but you have to put out the decoys, which means a boat or waders or both or getting soaked at the beginning of a long, cold day.

Solution: A tennis ball mimicking a tennis ball filled with steak juice but actually injected with cement. Throw the ball to where you want the decoys—the dogs swim out, but the ball has sunk so the dogs spend all day tipping up looking at the ball on the bottom (talk about realistic).

Problem: Then, at the end of the day, you have to collect the decoys—boat, waders, wet again.

Solution: Not so with dogs—just call them—roll a steak-juice-filled tennis ball on the bank, and then toss it into the car.

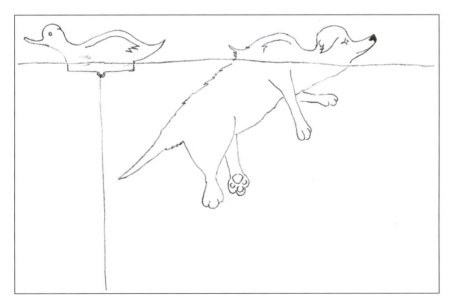

The Baltimore duck head

When the ducks come to the BDHLD dogs, the dog is already there when you shoot it, which saves time because the duck practically falls into the dog's mouth and it delivers to hand. No messy splashing or leaping out of the boat, and most importantly, no smelly, monsooning dog in the boat.

We of the fishing/hunting dog world have been working on strains of BDHLD dogs with different species of duck-shaped heads. Nobody has ever been able to breed a dog to get a perfect head—say for teal or Canada geese. We have had some good luck breeding a dog that looks like a duck "tipped" up. (But more on that later, when you get to "making your own dog.")

Small Digression: Baltimore Duck Heads Saved by the Nova Scotia Duck Tollers

At one point in the last century, there was an effort to register the Baltimore duck heads—I remember asking why would anyone want to do that? Well it turns out that the hunters were faced with a real problem. Fifty years had gone by and they hadn't invented a new breed of dog that was no good. Thus even though the duck heads were so successful, they thought they might have to sacrifice one dog to keep up with their registration requirements.

However, in the nick of time, they got a breed that failed well, which was the Nova Scotia duck tolling dog.

The duck tolling dog works very much the same way as the Baltimore duck heads—just a little different. The idea with them is that you teach them to chase tennis balls, too. Then you inject a tennis ball with cement so that it sinks, just like with the Baltimore duck heads. When you throw the tennis ball out where you want the ducks to come, the dog goes to the spot and looks for the ball, splashing all around trying to dive down to where the ball is.

The theory was that the ducks way-down-the-other-end of the pond think the dog is a fox because it has been bred to look like a fox. And they think the fox is killing and eating ducks, perhaps some of their friends and relatives. So the ducks fly down to see if any of their friends or relatives are being eaten, and *bang*! The hunter shoots them, of course trying not to shoot the dog at the same time.

I don't know where hunters get these ideas. The dogs were such miserable failures, they were only good for pets—great at playing tennis ball chase with children. They were almost immediately registered as a breed in Canada and they were so bad that someone told me they also had to be registered in America, too.

The good news is they fulfilled the fifty-year hunting dog breed quota and the Baltimore duck heads still go unnoticed.

Some of the more perspicacious punt gunners noticed that fish were collecting under the Baltimore duck heads on bright days. And thus it started. Many a punt gunner, under duckless skies, would fish a dog. The smarter ones began to realize that as duck populations dwindled, they could supplement their incomes with fish, and they began to breed those dogs that attracted fish. The curly retriever coat remained tight against the dog even when wet, and looked very much like tree bark. (Not to be confused with tree barking, another phenomenon perfected by hunters in their dogs.) The best ones even smelled like fish, a trait that also has been passed along to our present-day retrievers.

Thus the log dogs germinated. When punt gunning as a commercial venture was outlawed, duck-headed dogs still had value for their shadows, and so they were still bred, but now they were bred for fishing. At first, it required great skill by the fishermen to get these dogs to look and behave like a log and not a duck. But over the years, log dogs have evolved nicely from animal quackers to cheery oaks.

Because of these dogs' stubbly legs, pudgy bodies, duck-like heads, and fishy smell, some thought the log dogs were in fact basset hounds. Given the enunciation of fisherman, this was soon corrupted to bassin hound, a breed name by which log dogs are commonly known. Following the widespread acceptance of this name, a reformation of the mythologies and assumptions shrouding the breed led to the dogma that they were bred intentionally for largemouth fishermen. This is now true, but it was not so originally.

Bassin hounds are a distinct variety of gillie dogs, and are headed for breed status. Shadiness is their cardinal virtue, but unlike the other raft breeds (for example, floating mat dogs), bassins always take an active interest in finding fish. They float slowly toward a fish and, when it is underneath them, they blow easily out of their nostrils, making little bubbles[28] that rise to the surface and signal the alert fisherman where to cast.

Fishing Your Log Dog

Fishers of largemouth bass set their dogs in the shallows along banks, arranged in realistic fashion. Once the dog is in position, it should take an active interest in the mimicry. If the dog can sink just slightly at the tail end, it achieves the half submerged, waterlogged look that is highly desirable in some locations. I have never seen the variety that sinks at the head end.

A conscientious log-dogger constantly checks on his dogs. In reservoirs with rising and falling water, the dog's position has to be constantly monitored. Many a fisherman who has set up ten or more log dogs has lost one because it drifted,

---

[28] Environmentalists long thought these were methane bubbles. Even though bassins do emit pure methane from one end, this can be strictly controlled through diet. No conscientious fisherman would add to global warming by feeding his dog improperly.

unnoticed, off the bank and ended up at some paper mill. The fact that your dog could end up as the front page of *The New York Times* should be enough to make you pay attention. A map takes time to make but it is well worth it in the end. Attention to detail can save the angler many hours slogging through rafts of logs looking for his favorite working dog. Some of the best log mimics have been retrieved by campers and, unfortunately, used for roasting marshmallows. Down south, alligators can be a problem and the fisherman can end up with a bunch of petrified dogs.

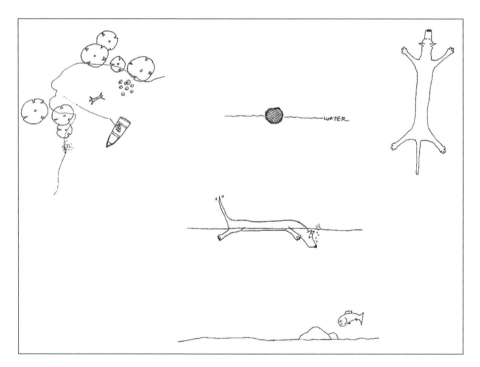

Log dog in action—conformation standard

Naming a Log Dog

Fly-fishing log-doggers tend to give their dogs names like Driftwood, Sandalwood, or Lincoln. You see their registration forms inscribed with the likes of "Champion Dreadknot of Basswood." Lady fishermen usually call their log dogs Twiggy, Splinters, or Yule. Of course, coarse fishermen like my friend Stan call theirs Bark, which turned out to be literally a worldwide disaster.

Another Small Digression

Here is how it happened. Like most people, Stan doesn't know why dogs bark. Dogs bark because other dogs bark. The dog up the road barks, and then your dog barks, and then the dog way down the road barks. So Stan has this dog called Bark. Merrily, Stan sticks his head out the front door and yells "Bark!" and of course his dog Bark is obedient to his master and barks. Then the dog down the road barks, and the dog way down the road barks, and the dog way, way down the road barks.

At 1100 feet/second it takes the barking chain 72 minutes to reach the Mississippi River and, on a good day with a fair wind, about 5 hours and 20 minutes to reach California and, at the same time, all the Mexican dogs have started barking. I kid you not—do you realize how close the Aleutian Islands are to Russia and all of Asia? If my calculations are correct, the barking could go around the world and in a mere 32 hours—the dog up the road would be barking and then Stan's dog and then it starts again with the dog down the road and way down the road. God knows what is happening in South America or Africa, even. It is hard to know if barking ever ends. It's a wonder that anybody gets any sleep.

There is a knack to selecting log puppies. Don't pick the runt, no matter how cute it is: always keep that old song in mind and be sure you "gitta long little doggie." (Humming it is helpful during the selection process to keep you focused on

A cord of log dogs

log scales.) Stan and I had a great log dog once. Butt always looked like he was on the way to the pulp mill. He became totally immersed in his role as a log. He was truly one with the environment. I loved to sit and watch him in the morning. Turtles crawled up on his back to sun themselves, waiting for their breakfast, while I waited for mine. If fish didn't come around, Butt drifted slowly over to them.

Oh, and they can be stacked like cordwood.

STRINGER SPANIELS

The biggest difference (probably to be legalistic about it I should say, "in my opinion"), the biggest and dumbest difference between modern hunters-with-dogs and fishers-with-dogs, in my opinion, is: hunters are the kind of people whose dogs find the game; the dog is the one that retrieves it, and the hunter person is the one who carries the game home. The fisher person, on the other hand, has the thrill of finding the fish and providing the expertise for capturing the fish, and his dog carries the fish home. This, naturally, is what stringer spaniels are for.

In early times, before this breed arose, hunters and fishers both carried their trophies home, and they had the same basic techniques. Hunters clung religiously to these traditions. At first, they tied a string around the game and carried it over the shoulder. This system was pretty good, except that other hunters, seeing game going through the forest in this position, were never quite sure if the game was afoot or if it was dead. Often they would shoot it again to make sure.

This led to the development of the pocket. After a hunter shot a pheasant, for example, he would put it in the large pocket in the back of his coat. Then other hunters could tell whether the pheasant was dead or not, by smelling the pocket. You could smell the pocket up to several years later if you were curious whether the pheasant was still dead. Getting deer into a pocket is more of a problem and hunters still drag a deer around, or better yet—use carts, which get the deer up where it can be seen, making it easier for other hunters to shoot it over and over until all concur that it is dead.

Fishermen have their equivalents: stringers (more on these below), vests with pockets, and cute little baskets called creels. These wicker hampers have a little teeny hole in the top so fly-fishermen can slip their fish in without even opening the cover. Creels have become standard equipment for flyfishermen, part of the uniform, so to speak, and even catch-and-release fisher-men are still required to carry one.

Now, Stan used to carry a stringer most of the time. A stringer is basically a length of "unbreakable" line that the successful fisher threads between the fish's gills and through its mouth. He is then supposed to tie the two ends to the boat and lower the strung fish into the water. Stringers come in many designs, from the very simple and easy to use to the much more difficult and nearly impossible to use. This latter is a chain with huge side-branching safety pins. Stan seems to require one thing of his stringers: they must sink if you drop one over the side. Furthermore, they must be so heavy they will convey all the fish to the deepest part of the pond. His stringers provide us with hours of fun playing grapple. Stanley eventually came up with the idea that we should get a stringer spaniel. As usual, as long as I found the dog and trained the dog, he'd pay half and I could keep it at my place.

Stringer spaniels have curly coats about the consistency of Velcro® tape. The fact that fish are scaly and have gill covers and gill arches and gill rakes means it is really easy to stick one to the dog. Just take the fish by its tail and middle and shove the head into the dog's fur. Any place will do, as long as there's not already a fish there. For some people, this is not a problem. I like to balance my fish across the dog. Regardless, nothing gives me more satisfaction than watching a stringer come home at night, loaded.

The Origin of the Stringer Spaniel

Many famous breeds have obscure origins.[29] The stringer spaniel is no exception. I'd always assumed that the stringer was a derivative of the log dogs. Log dogs hang around in the water and have those bark-mimicking coats. It seems to me it would be easy for evolution to make a little leap to a full-blown stringer. But, I must admit, I really don't know where they came from or who made the connection that you could stick a fish to a dog.

---

[29] Most of these now-famous but once-obscure dogs are hunting dogs. I think this is because hunters don't realize what they have if it is working okay. It is only when the dog is no good and they have to get it registered that they look for its origins.

I asked Stanley one time where he first heard about them. He immediately went into mumble mode and said something like, he hadn't heard about them and thought I'd made a mistake, but he had really said, "springer spaniel." That didn't make any sense to me because Stanley couldn't stick a fish to a springer even with potato glue.

Choosing and Using Your Stringer Spaniel

Stringers come in all sizes, and you should get a size that suits your typical fishing experience. If you are like me, get a very large stringer spaniel. If you are like Stan, you should get a dog with a steel wool tongue for polishing the utensils and chisel-sharp front teeth for getting the home fries off the pan. If you are a flyfisherman and don't like bringing a lot of fish home,[30] then a toy stringer is good enough. I always think it's cute when you open up someone's creel and there is a creel stringer. The little tyke sticks her head out of the tiny hole in the top and watches the flipping of the poly horsehair. Such dogs are categorized as second stringers.

Stringers can be tethered to the side of the boat during the day and fish can be added to them right in the water. This keeps both the fish and dog fresh so they don't start smelling. In small ponds, I don't even tie my dog. When we move the boat to a new set of lily pads, the dog follows by himself later on. It's more interesting for the dog if it is allowed to

---

[30] People who like to catch-and-release or practice other forms of not bringing fish home can stop reading this section and go directly to the chapter on spotter dogs (page 121). Spotter dogs can help you find the fish to catch so that you might actually need a stringer spaniel in the future.

The stringer spaniel

explore on its own. But it should know to hustle right over when someone yells, "Fish on!" Unless that someone is a fly-fisherman who gives the fish a sporting chance and practices catch-and-release often almost simultaneously.

If you work your dog with the free-float technique, you should try to put the same number and size of fish on each side of the dog. Don't, for instance, put all the big ones on one side. Since the fish are still alive, they continue to swim even though they are stuck to the dog, and they can exert considerable vector forces that interfere with his unidirectional swimming: having all the big fish on one side may require the dog to swim in one great big circle to get to you. In an extreme case, the dog might just pivot *in situ*.

A fatal "fault" in some stringers is the rolling gene, widely exhibited by not-so-well-bred stringer spaniels. This behavior, shared with many non-stringer breeds, was unfortunately ignored by some irresponsible breeders. One breeder actually selected for this behavior, trying to turn it into a virtue, by claiming that the dog is loading its own fish. Like many bad genes, the fish-rolling behavior has swept through the dog world like a bona fide genetic disease. Just let my son Tigger's dog outside and she'll travel miles to find dead fish and pick them up by Velcroing. She is usually successful unless she meets a porcupine first. Most dogs instinctively know that dead fish should be Velcroed. This fish-rolling behavior sometimes gets so bad that several once-fine working breeds have had to be registered.

Stan always teaches his dogs to roll over on command, something that puzzles me. "What on earth do you have in mind?" I query. "What practical value could rolling on command have for a dog?" Stan mumbles something about if the dog should burst into flames and you're not able to find a heavy blanket. After Stan trained our first stringer, Threads, the dog mushed 250 fish into perch purée. I think Stan learned his lesson about rolling on command.

Digression: Hatch Matching Spaniels

Earlier, I introduced you to the Ghilly on the Gary who had two Labrador retrievers, one black lab and one yellow lab, from which he plucked the hair out appropriately to match the hatch. The guy was a genius and that led Stan and me to a great idea: why couldn't you breed up a bunch of stringer spaniels with different colored coats, such that you could snip or pluck their hair for flies? We tried it and it worked okay, but if you had a hatch and didn't have a dog with the right color hair, you're stuck. We solved that by taking lots of stringer spaniels fishing (that didn't bother me of course), each of a different color—a veritable pack of spaniels.

Well, not everybody likes to go fishing with a pack of dogs, especially if you are fishing from a canoe. For me, the answer was simple—get a bigger canoe. One of our fishing buddies, Craig Kling from Wyoming, thought he knew how to solve the packing problem. Craig saw an opportunity with a hybridization program and set up one of the most complex breeding programs you could imagine—first single dogs with two colors, then single dogs with four colors, then eight, then sixteen, and so on.

That meant you could have one dog that had small patches of different color, different lengths for making streamers, different hair diameters and curliness. Unbelievable what you can do with a good breeding program, some random genetic combinations, and stringer spaniels eager to participate in genetic transfer at any opportunity.

Here, I'll let Craig tell you in his own few but brief words:

The Lowdown on the Hatch-Matching Spaniels (HMS)

The multi-hued HMS has been selectively bred to support those fly-fisher-persons (FFPs) who take portable fly-tying equipment to the stream, lake, pond, or sea to match-the-hatch currently occurring on the water and theoretically being favored by fish at that time. This extremely devoted match-the-hatch FFPs (MHFFPs) often spend more time gathering and observing the hatch and attempting to match it than actually fishing. However, if you are not catching any fish, tying flies makes the time go quicker. It is often overlooked in the frenzy to tie an exact match-the-hatch fly (MHF) of the moment on a suitable-sized hook before another insect species decides to hatch, requiring a completely different fly.

The HMS provide the MHFFP with a complete source of fly-tying material (FTM) of a multitude of colors, textures, and length, and curl right or left on different sides of the dog at hand (or at heel). MHFFPs are divided into two groups: the pluckers (P as in PMHFFP) that pull the hair out of the dog directly and the snippers (S also SMHFFP) that remove the desired hair with a quick snip of scissors.

HMSs have been bred in two distinct types depending on whether the HMFFP is a splitter favoring a couple or even a pack of usually min-iature HMSs with individuals yielding variation of FTMs, or a lumper favoring a larger HMS with enough surface area to support a wider variety of FTM on the one specimen, thereby reducing the need for a large pack of HMSs.

While most HMS are eager to accompany HMFFPSs when they see the fishing and fly-tying gear being loaded in a vehicle, the PMHFFP's MHSs have a tendency to hide. They quickly learn to disappear when one or more fishing buddies (FBs) show up after having been plucked naked on a previous fishing trip by the HM supplying flies to all MHFFPFBs on a very diverse hatch day.

Tight lines—Craig

We should introduce Craig to Barnaby Porter. There is a caution though. If you are plucking your stringer too often, there might not be enough hair to stick your fish onto.

HMS (avoidance behavior)

Naming Your Hatch-Matching Spaniel

Sample names are HMS Victory, HMS Royal Oak, plus you get cutesy variations like Muttney on the HMS Bownty. You hear PHMSs frequently called Patches and many SHMSs are called Motely after a long trip with MHFFP's FBs.

Chapter 9

The Fish Spotter Dogs

Like the gillies, the fish spotters are one of the two main classifications of fishing dogs. While some of the ghillie dogs (notably the bassin hound and the more intelligent floating mat dogs) have some spotting abilities, fish spotters are specifically named for their acute looking skills. Fishermen think they are named for their marking abilities, as the name "spotter" implies. This is confusing to many non-dog experts and hunters and to AKC representatives who give talks at annual meetings. Let me try to clear up this confusion between sporting dogs and spotting dogs.

Often, in the field, a hunter will say "Mark!" to his pointer when the dog looks in a meaningful way at say (usually), a bird. To "Mark!" in human-to-dog sense is to use the nose to look.

In this case, the dog's nose directs the human's eyes. If the dog smells a bird, the human looks in the direction of the smell until he comes upon the bird. At that point, he yells "Mark!" and the dog tries to claim the bird. But the bird flies up and the hunter has to shoot it so the dog can reclaim and eat it, which is why it wanted to claim it in the first place. The dog interprets the command "Mark!" in the "claim as mine" category of behavior.[31]

Contrast this behavior with what wolves do. Like dogs, wolves chase deer, but unlike dogs, they do not mark birds. Wolves mark territories ("this area is mine"). Now, to train a bird dog to mark a bird the same way a wolf claims his territory goes against everybody's best instincts. Wolves claim territories by marking the boundaries with a secret message system. When wolves turned into dogs, they kept the same code books, but since dogs have moved into the suburbs where there are fewer trees, they mark telephone poles, fire hydrants, and coffee tables to signal the edges of their territory. Since there are fewer of these scent posts in the suburbs than there were trees in the forest, more messages have to be left on each one.

A pointer marks birds with its nose. Therein the similarity between wolves and dogs breaks down, because wolves smell where they have been marking. But if dogs marked birds as territorial boundaries, then what? Thus, bird dogs are totally confused when they point a bird and the hunters say "Mark!" and so the dogs usually revert to chasing deer.

---

[31]   One of the best Chessie trainers I know is named Mark, which makes a hunt really confusing.

When hunters say, "Mark!" what they really mean is "Jump!"—"Jump, dog, where you are smelling." If wolves jumped where they smelled, they'd kill themselves. All the breeds of hunting dogs have figured out the differences except the red (Irish) setters, which continue to jump into trees.

The fish spotter dogs aren't like the coffee-table markers. They don't mark by making a spot; they spot by looking. They look at the fish. The fisherman looks where the dog is looking and there is a fish. Fish spotters don't smell.

Regardless of what anybody tells you, dogs can't smell under water. They smell everyplace else, but not under water.

Digression about Talking while Fishing and Rocky Pointers

My favorite fish spotter breed is the rocky pointer, which is probably the best of the pike pointers. I started using them because electronic fish finders have been a constant problem for me. It's frustrating to work one if your fishing buddy is Stan.

Fishing is one of those times when two guys can go out in a boat and quietly do their thing. There is no need to talk. The best fishing buddies (Stan is mine) can go for days without saying a word. But with one of those electronic fish finders in the boat, the peace of the wilderness, the stealth of the stalk, is shattered. "How deep is it now?"

"Is it still three feet?" "See anything on the scope?" "How deep is it now?" "Move back to three feet!"

I finally had to get Stan his own depth finder. Other fisherman probably wondered why my modest fourteen-foot aluminum boat had two fairly serious depth finders in it. The reasoning was Stan could look at his own depth finder and all would be quiet again. But it was not to be. "What does your depth finder say?" "Huh; mine says two-and-a-half feet." It was another one of those cases where, to save our relationship, we got rid of the electronic fish finders and got another dog.

PIKE POINTER

It is exciting seeing a pike pointer at work: he stands in the boat sticking his head over the side and under water. When his tail stiffens and starts to vibrate, and his front leg draws up against his chest in a point, you know right where the keeper fish is! Well, you almost know where it is.

With pike pointers, there is a problem the average pheasant hunter doesn't have. With upland field dogs, you know exactly where the bird is by projecting an imaginary line from between the dog's eyes, bisecting the nostrils and on down the line out to meet the ground—where, sometimes, there is a bird. Good dogs look where they are pointing while bad dogs point where they are looking. Most hunters don't know the difference.

But because of the physical principles that govern ground, light, and water, pike pointers are not looking where you think they are looking. Unless you are jigging for flounders, fish are not usually on the ground, but rather suspended between the ground (under water, the technical term is "bottom") and the surface of the water.

Here is the main point. Under water, the imaginary line is even more imaginary than if it were out of the water. Therefore, you have to make some calculations, based on the dog's point of view, to determine the real depth and direction of the fish. Using the imaginary line ploy, you need to know the distance along the imaginary line A to the fish.

Pike pointing—the von Frisch principle and more

When your imaginary line gets to the fish, project it straight up so that it intersects the surface at right angles (imaginary line B). The length of imaginary line B is equivalent to the depth of the fish. You now know how deep to run your lure.

This book is not written for beginners, but if you are a beginner, realize that most manufacturers publish the depths at which the lure runs right on the package, and if you are a clever person, your package is in your lure box. This is the manufacturer's response to deep ecology: it not only helps you run at the proper depth, but keeps you from littering.

Although you now know how deep to run the lure, believe it or not, you don't know where the fish is. That's because when you drew imaginary line B straight from the fish to the surface, you assumed that if you went straight back down B, you would find the fish. But you're wrong. The fish at the end of the imaginary line was an imaginary fish. The real fish is a few feet away. You need to calculate the real, as distinct from the perceived, direction.[32] The dog has his head under water and is looking directly at the fish. You can't see the fish. If you could, you wouldn't need the dog. The dog is looking at a different place than you are, even though you are both trying to look at the same thing—the fish. Your projected imaginary line from the dog's eyes across its nose on out into the depths is not a real imaginary line, but an *imaginary*

---

[32]   Many of my students have to reread this section several times so don't feel bad if you don't quite get it the first time.

imaginary line. You have to calculate the difference between the imaginary line you are imagining and the imaginary line you should be imagining.

Example: The dog's imaginary line (from now on called

Between the ears calculation

IL) is exactly at right angles to the surface. This means that the fish is under the boat. You should use some kind of jig. Simple enough, but there is a complication that has to be accounted for in all calculations other than the perpendicular illustration.

Normally, the pike pointer's point will be correct, that is, his IL is accurate, but his head is under water and yours shouldn't be. This means you have to calculate the angle of refraction. Surface refraction or the bending of the light happens when light goes from an aqueous medium to a gaseous medium, for example, from the water to the air above it.

It helps to know some geometry, trigonometry, and if the boat is moving, calculus. The formula is based on the angle that your head is displaced from the obtuse angle the dog is pointing. If you are standing right over the dog, then this is no problem because your IL is theoretically in the same direction as the dog's, except yours is running along the surface and his is under water. That means you can't calculate the depth of the fish. That, in conjunction with refraction, also means your IL is longer than his IL, even though the actual distance is the same for both of you. This is one of those cases where you do not question your dog: the dog knows best.

To say this is no problem is a slight misstatement. If you are standing right over the dog and the dog has its head underwater, leaning over the side of the boat, that means you and the dog are on the same side of the boat and therefore both your heads are over the same side of the boat: you may experience capsizing boat syndrome. There are two solutions to this problem: 1) get a gyro dog as big as you and the pointer combined, or 2) learn how to compute the refraction angles. Please look at the illustration for an example of a refraction angle.

To return to the depth problem, which some of you mathematicians probably thought I was avoiding, when you have the true IL calculated, you have to compute the distance to the fish. This is because you need to know not only how deep the fish is, but how far it is, since in most cases you can't see it. Both distances are easier to determine than the refraction angles, because they can't be computed mathematically; but both can be estimated. If the initial angle is small and the bottom is shallow, then accuracy is not very important. It is when the bottom is sixty feet away and the fish are suspended at ten feet that we have a problem.

But from watching these dogs, I learned a little trick. A pike pointer positions its tail directly over its back and wags it in figure eights.[33] The speed of the tail wag is an approximation of how far the fish is from the dog's nose. You must remember that there is an inverse correlation between the rate of tail movement and the length of the IL. Fast moving tails mean short ILs, but slow moving tails may only mean anticipation of a fish that has not appeared yet. With a little practice, you'll become an expert at interpreting the dog's signals.

To gauge the distance more accurately, check which part of the tail is wagging. If it's just the tip, the fish is very close; the whole tail wagging from the base means the fish is far away. How far? Well, I find that the point of wag corresponds to the length of the IL. In other words, if a dog is wagging halfway down the tail, then the fish is halfway down the Potential Imaginary Line (PIL), which is the distance the dog can see under water.

(It is so complicated that a guy named Carl von Frisch got the Nobel Prize for figuring this out.)

---

[33] People are always wondering what dogs mean by wagging their tails. The answer is, "How long is it until supper?"

The PIL varies with water conditions. At the beginning of the fishing day, stick your head under water and have your fishing buddy pull out a measuring tape. When you can't see his hand any more, record the distance: this is your base PIL. Remember that a dog can see slightly farther than a human, and of course changes in cloud cover and water turbulence will change the PIL hourly.

Dozing when the dog is working, or not making the calculations speedily, is unfair to the dog. Pike pointers who get stuck on point need attention much more quickly than an English pointer who can't shake a bobwhite. Natural selection has operated much more quickly on pike pointers than on English pointers, which is why the former have never required registration with a local kennel club.

Training your Pike Pointer

Training a pike pointer is no more difficult than training the average red setter. All the standard equipment is used.

Step 1. Raise the puppies chewing on tennis balls with a fish painted on the side. (It doesn't matter what smelly substance you injected them with because dogs can't smell under water, but I prefer fish juices in cod liver oil—besides, it is healthful to growing puppies.)

Step 2. When the dog is old enough, using a marked line, cast the stinky fish-pictured tennis ball injected with liquid cement out in the water and let it sink. The dog will stick its head under water and watch it come back as you retrieve it. Practice retrieving it at different rates and watch carefully the angle of the dog's head, while also watching its tail wag. You might write down the particulars of the tail wag as each of the line marks comes by. As you get more sophisticated, you might stop retrieving every once in a while, letting the tennis ball sink and watch the dog's head follow it down. If you had a marked floating tape measure, you could note the angle of the head and the distance the ball sinks while noting how far from the boat that is. Then you might repeat the process with a dead fish injected with the cod liver oil mixture and a little cement to help it sink. Many professional pike pointer trainers do this photographically. Thus, when you buy a pre-trained or started pike pointer, it usually comes with a DVD.

Step 3. Pretend to cast the tennis ball or dead fish. The rest is history.

Dear Stanley, who is the kind of guy who never reads the instructions on the packages, has developed his own system for training a pike pointer. He uses a twenty-four-foot davit, so he can lower a fish in full view of the dog. Stan starts the dog at home, pointing fish in the aquarium.

When the dog can't keep his eyes off the fish tank, then Stan hangs the tank off the back porch with some monofilament. Stan slowly lowers the aquarium into his swimming pool. After that, every time Stan lets the dog out, the dog sees the fish line going into the pool and, thinking that his

Pike pointer—home training

favorite aquarium is at the end, it (the dog) sticks its head under water. Finally Stan just keeps the monofilament in the pool and the dog keeps sticking his head in the pool looking for the aquarium.

Eventually, we blindfold the dog for the car ride, and keep the blindfold on until we get to the middle of the lake. Then we dangle a line over the side of the boat. When the blindfold is removed, the dog sees the line, thinks there is a box with a fish in it under the water, and begins to look for it. You've won. "Good boy, clever fellow, well done."

Naming Pointer Dogs

Pike pointers and rocky pointers usually are given regal names like their terrestrial counterparts. English pointers always seem to have baronial names that never quite sit right for me. I believe dog names should follow a theme—a theme that says something about the pointer and its behavior. Perhaps I'd combine this with giving them names that speak of our First American traditions. How about, Chiefly-Stuck-on-Point?

Thematic variations might include Brave-Can't-Find-the-Bird or Eat-the-Bird. Once you know the breed, well, the possibilities are endless.

The tradition carries over into pike pointers, but in a different way. The aqueous environments they work in should be respected. Samples for rocky pointers are Too-Darn-Cold, Two-Fish, or Take-a-Breath. Some people use these dogs strictly in salt water applications and name the dogs accordingly—for example, Rusty. My best dog could keep his head under for a long time and I named it Old Blue. And he was a good dog, too.

Pet Pointers

I promised to say something about using pike pointers as pets and show dogs. Again, field trials are fairly easy, but in the show ring they just look like any other dog out of water. Pet is a problem all in itself. You take the dog to dog-training class and they can learn to sit and stay as well as any other dog. But I imagine at about the fifth time, you'll call the dog trainer and say, "He has his head stuck in the water dish again." People never seem to realize that you can't stamp out instincts.

Chapter 10

The Dogfish Dogs

The dogfish dogs (DFD) are breeds of dogs that actually catch fish all by themselves. There are two kinds: 1) those that sit and wait, and 2) those that pursue and catch fish. Both kinds are more difficult to train than the baildales and the already-bailed-dales. Each of the dogfish breeds needs to be taught to deliver to hand and, like many of the hunter's retrievers, one has to be very critical of dogs with hard mouths. DFDs that eat the quarry in the water before delivering to hand pose unique training problems. There are some advantages of the dogfish over your regular terrestrial scoop-up-the-game dogs—mainly, they don't chase deer.

ANGLER DOG

Angler dogs are descended from do-it-yourself pike point-ers although they look more like the pikes than the pointers. They look like a cross between a pit bull and the angler fish. An angler fish is an ugly critter with a big mouth, with lots of teeth and something like a rubber worm dangling from the roof of the mouth. This worm mimic is a loose hanging organ that looks like how the top of your mouth feels after you bite into a right-out-of-the-oven pizza. The angler fish sits with its mouth hanging open, waiving the pizza flap. The first anchovy that nibbles the dangle gets a final lesson in "stimulus and response." The mouth, containing a million teeth, snaps shut. There is no such thing as a have-a-heart angler fish, nor are there catch-and-release angler fish.

The angler dog—fishing

Angler dogs don't have the pizza flap, but rather a modified (some might say deformed) tongue. The tongue looks like an Arkansas crawler (an earthworm): it is shaped like a thick brown corkscrew. In its relaxed position, it hangs out of the dog's mouth, and it can also be withdrawn into the dog's mouth in a series of little jerks, giving it a lifelike motion that is attractive to fish. It also helps if they have really bad breath, like manure pile extract.

The lifelike jerks are a result of the panting muscles. Normal dog tongues go in and out when a dog pants; this facilitates the action of the saliva groove (*cavia linguini*) which runs down the center of the tongue. Angler dogs don't have this trenched tongue, and they can only pant under water (more on that in a minute).

Angler Dog Appearance and Standards

Angler dogs are serious dogs, and not for everybody. Their faces are piranha-like, with uncountable needle-like teeth. Often there are teeth where you wouldn't expect dogs to have teeth. The teeth in the upper jaw are skewed slightly from those in the lower jaw: this is a major plus in the breed. If their teeth lined up perfectly, they would slice the fish in half, the way a bird dog sometimes crush-bites a bird.

The best angler dog tongue color is earthworm (naturally). The second best color (though more rare) is white. Glow white is especially great for night fishing for bullheads. Considerable variation in color is allowed for show dogs. As usual, some of the show breeders have missed the point of why angler dogs' tongues are important. Last year, a chap took best of breed with a dog that had a camouflage-colored tongue.

The tongue should be not only colored like an earthworm, but shaped like an earthworm, as well. It should be long, round, and narrow, with a clearly segmented appearance. Lateral constrictions producing clearly demarcated segments are acceptable. The tongue must never be normal. A Scruffs judge once disqualified a dog with an earthworm tattoo on a normal tongue.

The nose of the angler dog is a modified bulldog shape. The original bulldogs had nostrils pointing dorsally, allowing the dog to breathe while its teeth were buried in the deep warm folds of the bull's neck. The angler dog is similarly designed, but the nostrils are more pronounced and farther back on its snout. The nostrils have migrated with the rostrum, to a position almost between the eyes. Here is a dog that smells exactly the way it looks. My goal is to have nostrils right between the ears and shaped like the blow hole of a dolphin.

All breeds of dogs have a twitch or sniff muscle around the nostrils. This allows them to sample air in little pulses, increasing the concentrations of smells. These constrictoid muscles also prevent entry of flies, which are curious as to why dogs smell that way. In the angler dog, the dorsally-situated nostrio-constrictoid muscles are modified into a cartilaginous flap, which stops water from flowing into the dog's head if the nostroids descend below the aqueous plane. Otherwise, because of its unique anterior position of the nostrils, if it weren't for the nostroids, the dog would have water on the brain.

Like beagles (see page 35), angler dogs come in different sizes. For general purposes, the popular #2 Victor with padded jaws is best, though bear trap models with multiple serrations are also available. Stan likes the .5 Oneida for miniature baleen anglers, while I tend to like the 10x sizes. Then again, he prefers quality perch, pan-size fish. Stan finds cleaning small fish a challenge, so he catches a lot of them.

Major Digression: Angler Dog Physiology and Drool Syndrome

As I have hinted, the driving principle of a good angler dog is temperature control. Just about everybody knows that normal dogs cool themselves by panting. Pants come in pairs, technically the inhale and exhale, also known as sucking and blowing, to cause air to flow over the moistened tongue. It is mostly the exudate that we are concerned with here. (I'll save the inudate for the advanced course.)

Dog exudate is a gaseous vapor that is specially adapted to take heat and highly toxic chemicals away from the dog. You know immediately when the dog is in the toxic chemical phase of the cycle, but heat transfer is undetectable unless the dog is on fire (see rolling, page 115). The exudate transfers heat from the tongue to the surroundings. This process causes a deterioration of the molasses-like salivary formula, which the dog fortifies by eating grass and rolling in fish (again, see page 115). The salivary formula can be adjusted to essence of skunk oil, which you doggy people know is popular with most of our domestic breeds. Tincture of Abyssinian civet is a favorite of my dogs, while my son Tigger's dogs specialize in northern pike paste.

Dog saliva is unique in other ways. Production is in a pair of organs, the *grandulosus salivalarium* complex. God only knows why they are paired. In most domestic dogs, these two organs make twice as much cooling fluid as necessary, to store perhaps in case of emergencies; for instance, when a hot spell is unforecasted and the dog is caught in, rather than under, the house. Each *grandulosus* duct has a bivalve, which operates with clam-like precision to release the excess exudate continuously into the environment. The *grandulosus salivalarium* has nonstick walls to prevent salivary molasses from sludging before it reaches the outside of the dog.

The *cavia linguini,* or saliva groove, trenches the medial portion of the tongue from the *grandulosus salivalarium* to the anterior edge (trench tongue). Its particular function is to mold the salivary molasses into long strings. Once a string has absorbed sufficient heat, the dog can release it (the heat-infested portions) in a gesture similar to that of an Argentinean *vaquero* catching an ostrich with a bola.

The technical term for the whole process is evapio-drooling (named for the Italian physiologist Lumbardo Evapio, 1870–1933). Evapio-drooling is the most common method of preventing boil-over in dogs. When dogs are thermally stressed, they place the cooling molasses on other portions of their bodies that feel hot. With small head shakes, they can reposition the entire contents of the *salivalarium* to the surface of their faces, thus increasing the surface area where evapio-cooling takes place. Hot dogs also redirect the flow of cooling fluid to their front paws and legs. Some dogs, such as Saint Bernards, can make a small muddy pond, or dog-walla, in which they lie.

My son Tigger's Chessies have perfected these techniques. Their evolutionary advancement is the combining of evapio-drooling with instinctive monsooning. This allows them to place the cooling drool on ceilings and walls, where it acts as organic air-conditioning: an adaptive breakthrough allows them to cool their environment rather than their body. Dogs could give us the solution to global warming.

As you can see, the key factor for hot dogs is surface area. In order for dogs to evapio-cool properly, they have to have gigantic tongues. I've seen dogs with tongues half the length of their bodies with great huge medial trenches full to the brim with refrigeration fluids. These dogs could practically freeze to death on a hot day.

The miracle of the angler dog lies in its small convoluted tongue with the surface area of an earthworm. No *grandulosus salivalarium,* no *cavia linguini,* no cooling molasses. The angler dog does not have enough tongue area for evapio-drooling to affect evapio-cooling. This condition is exacerbated in larger angler dogs; small dogs' tongues are the size of actual earthworms. But so are those of the large dogs. No matter what you do to a dog, you can't change the size of an earthworm.

Angler dogs solve the cooling problem by soaking their tongues in water. Water cools the tongue much faster than air, so keeping its tongue submerged in water allows the dog to pump hot blood through the earthworm at a more leisurely pace.

I love my anglers. When I come home at night, they don't even look up from their water dishes—they can't, for fear their tongues will come out of the water. They roll their eyes in my direction and I know they are happy to see me. They are not the kind of dog that jumps all over you, hosing down your suit with cooling molasses and drooly paws, like some Chessies. I have never been slimed by an angler dog.

As I go to hang up my coat, they do these funny little hops around the dish so they can continue to see me. Of course I know what they want. But in ritualistic fashion, I go about my business just as if I've forgotten all about treat time. They shuffle around their bowls again and watch me look at the mail.

Angler dog—tongue cooling

Then all of a sudden, I look up as if I just noticed them for the first time. Their stubby tails begin to wag. "Oh," I say, "Daddy's little dogfishes want their treat." The tail waggle is alarming now and I hustle to the refrigerator to bring the episode to a conclusion before their tongues come out of the water with all the excitement. They look happy as I bring the treats over, but the only noise you hear is their stubby tails thumping on the floor as I slip fresh ice cubes into their dishes.

Here are a couple of tips about angler dogs around the house: If all the water evaporates from their dish, the dogs will begin to migrate; as a precaution, I keep the bathroom door shut at all times. They can't bark while tongue-soaking, so smoke and burglar alarms should be well maintained. Finally, hiccups are more serious in this breed than in others; one good hiccup can siphon a bowl dry.

Fishing Your Angler Dog

Angler dogs' whole lives are about soaking their faces, and so they don't need much training. Simply place the dog on the edge of a river in your favorite wilderness fish-catching location and light up a cigar. The dog will immediately begin cooling its tongue, the fish will be attracted to the worm-like appendage, and the rest is inevitable. BANG! a strike, and BANG! the mouth snaps shut. When you have half a dozen dogs set out and a school of walleye passes by, life gets very exciting.

Some people think this is the greatest kind of fishing, because unlike other techniques, you don't have to do anything until the fish is actually caught. Lots of guys just sit around reading and smoking and having a nice day, until the dog comes up with a huge fish sticking out of its mouth. A snoozing fisherman might awaken to the pleasant call of his breakfast-cooking buddy: "Flag up!" But before you can pop the fish into the frying pan, it has to be extracted from the mouth of the angler dog. With the fish in the caught position, the dog can't open its mouth without help. There's a checklist of procedures to consult. First, nobody is going to think you are a sissy if you wear gloves—many an angler dog fisherman swears by Kevlar gloves, and I certainly recommend them for beginners. If you have a friend who is a pediatrician, a discarded set of forceps might be available.

Angler Dog—catching

I use the cashew method of extraction. Placing a dip net below the dog/fish union, blow cigar smoke between the eyes of the dog (remembering that is where the nostrils are), and cash-sheeew! the fish is sprung. Works every time! For non-smokers, the cashew reflex can sometimes be stimulated with a feather or perhaps by putting pollen on the dog's nostrils or . . . some fisherpeople use a beekeeper's smoker. Or simply have a fishing buddy who smokes—that's what fishing buddies are for, isn't it?

I often set my anglers first thing in the morning before Stan gets up. That way there is often something else to stick to the pan besides potatoes. In this high-cholesterol phase of human evolution, fish can be an important source of High Density Lipo Protein for the late morning angler.

You must bear in mind, though, that fish taken by and from angler dogs have to be prepared differently than fish taken by other forms of fish retrieval. Angler-caught fish are the equivalent of ground round, and your breakfast will be made up of fish patties from the same parts of a fish as a hot dog is from a cow. The good news is that your dressing percentage is higher than if you were doing pure fillets. Angler dog–caught fish are more purée than that. Stan doesn't seem to mind; he manages to blend the fish in with everything else in an unnoticeable way.

Naming Angler Dogs with Special Attention to Some of the Old Favorites

Most of the time, I get annoyed at what people name their angler dogs. The names always seem to be evil, violent, or just plain sick. Stan had one he named Squash, and he'd wander around singing, "I got a crush on you." I like names that not only reflect these dogs' sweet dispositions, but are appropriate to their function. So I started the theme of naming them after my favorite fishing lures.

My all-time favorite was little Cleo. She and her sister, Phoebe, were something else again. Phoebe worked deeper than little Cleo, and she wasn't afraid to get right to the bottom of a bass location. But, little Cleo really had action. Some angler dogs sit passively on the bank soaking their heads. They aren't really fishing; they are simply trying to be cool—any fish they get is by accident. But, little Cleo had the best case of wriggle you ever saw. She put a dance on the end of the old tongue that would be sinful to speak about in polite company. Also, she would cast about looking for the right spot. You could work her anywhere, as slow or fast as you wanted. Most anglers just head down the bank to the first place they come to. Not her. She'd collect a little cool in one place and then try to find a hot spot. And it paid off. Little Cleo caught fish.

Angler Dogs as Pets and Show Dogs

As pets, they are similar to pike pointers, monsooners, and bilge puppies in that they don't do anything. Some people think that makes a great pet and they should get one. They make lousy watchdogs because they cannot bark at burglars while soaking their tongues in ice water. Think of them as an aquatic rather than a terrestrial bulldog. If your little kids taught them to fetch tennis balls, then they would have to take up smoking. In the Special Dog Show ring, you are allowed an ice water dish on wheels.

TIPPUPS

Tippups may be the most highly evolved animal on Earth. In biological terms, that simply means they are better adapted to their niche than any other living animal. Perhaps they even approach perfection in a dog breed: certainly they are unique among the fishing dogs. Attention has been paid to every single detail of their conformation, a fine tuning that doesn't whistle in the wind.

Tippups are also the only breed I know that are named after a machine. Usually machines are named after dogs. Bulldogs are the symbol of doggedness, ergo the Mack truck; or fleetness, hence the Greyhound bus. Or ball teams are named after breeds: the Huskies, the Bulldogs, the Consolidated Hairless. Youngsters playing Softball have the Lassie League.

Tippups are specialists in the ice fishing division of angling sports. Whoever first got the idea that you could use a dog to replace the old-fashioned mechanical "tip-up" is lost to history. If you had to take a wild guess as to which group of sportsmen don't write a lot, naming ice fishermen would keep you in the contest. Ice fishermen are a cold bunch, and often they can't move their fingers for weeks. Similarly, their oral traditions can seldom be deciphered, though with a liberal application of lip camphor, you can occasionally get a frosted simile. Surely most ice fishermen would be lost if it weren't for the antifreeze they continually consume. I know guys who swore off drinking antifreeze and had to give up ice fishing.

Major Digression: Ice Fishing—the Ecological Approach

If you have never been ice fishing, you have no idea how cold it is out there in the middle of some godforsaken lake in February. Big frozen lakes have several ecological characteristics that only the expert fully appreciates. Take the words in order.

BIG. This is always an understatement. One rule of ice fishing is that you will find that the lake is much bigger than you thought. Mounting an expedition to the center of the lake is the stuff of National Geographic television specials. Why the center? Remember Stan's rules: if you are on shore, the fish are in the middle of the lake; if you are in the middle of the lake, the fish are on the far side; always cast as far as you can away from you. Well, the same rules apply in the winter, with a little modification—you'd look a little daft standing in the snow in a blizzard casting a frozen minnow out onto the ice. You must walk[34]—or drive—to the middle of the lake, and then to the far side. You never see anybody, no matter how naive and inexperienced, cut a hole in the ice beside the parking lot. Absolutely unheard of!

FROZEN. The other first rule of ice fishing is that ice fishing doesn't take place on nice days. Frozen is a word that has to be defined carefully. It would be easier here if I used technical and scientific terms. Lakes are large bodies of water. Lake water is layered, and each layer is a different temperature. The bottom of the lake is the hypolimnon. In the summer, the hypolimnon is the coldest layer of the lake, about 39°F. In the winter, it is

---

[34]   If you do anticipate walking, I suggest you consult with Amundsen Apparels, 3333 Itzcold Fiord St., Keerize, N.N. 0001 Norway.

the warmest layer of the lake, still 39°F. As you may have already deduced, the layers of a lake turn over from one season to the next; that is because wherever there is 39°F water, it goes to the bottom. (That is because water is most dense at 39°F—since fishermen are mostly made of water, they also are most dense at 39°F.)

The epilimnon is always on top, no matter what the temperature is. But, the epilimnon of summer becomes the warm hypolimnon of winter, even though the bottom remains the same temperature all year round.

In the summertime, fish are too hot at the top of the lake and go to the cool bottom (39°). In the winter, the top is too cold for fish, so they prefer the warm bottom (39°). Unless you are a fish, spending too much time in the hypolimnon at any season of the year is bad, so we must move on.

In a frozen lake, the top layers are somewhat anomalous. The lake is not exactly covered with ice. The lake is covered with wind, the hyperzephyrlon. The next layer below the wind layer and above the ice is very interesting: it consists of an unstable mixture of more or less wet shifting slush above the layer of rain water that lies on the ice below.

The hyperzephyrlon always contains water particles in one or more of three forms—snow, sleety wind, or rain. Each form of water sticks to the lake and insulates the adjoining layers from the form of water directly below it. Snow insulates the rain from on top of the ice from the colder wind above. Wind is the gaseous form of water and gets much colder than ice, which has a fixed temperature but is invariably cold.

The form of water particles in the hyperzephyrlon is inversely correlated with temperature: Arctic and Canadian cold fronts bring rain; warm Gulf air causes blizzard snow conditions. On nice days, you fish between the sleets.

It is complicated and difficult to explain. To put it in simple English (for the German edition, I'm sorry, but there isn't any simple German), each change of precipitation cakes on the ice with a frosting of snow on top, sandwiching the heavier rain water between the sleeting above and icing below. The rain percolates through the snow filter, settling on the ice that is floating on the top of the lake water, which is warmest at the bottom.

And now for a quick lesson on walking to the middle of the lake: step slowly. Pick a foot up and move it forward a short distance. Compact the snow with the bottom of your boot until you come to the sleet layer. Now shift your weight forward onto the sleet layer (sometimes called a crust because of its brittle and flaky quality). As your weight comes onto the crust, you shouldn't have any trouble breaking through. Your foot will quickly settle to the firm ice below the rain water. Wait a second until your boot fills up with pre-slush water, then repeat the process with the other foot. The further you go, the quicker it gets because you don't have to wait for your boots to fill up every time. The warmth of your feet will keep the in-boot water from freezing solid. Driving to the middle of the lake might be quicker, but walking back to get a tow truck would negate any time saved; the walk, however, does provide adequate exercise to make the experience worthwhile. Remember to take plenty of digestible antifreeze.

When you get to the middle of the lake, you must chop a hole in the ice. First, find a place where the ice is thin. This is usually under the pickup truck. Next, a hole must be cleared above the ice. The snow and sleet are easier to clear than the rain water, and fishermen often leave that where it is—chopping a hole underneath this water is not impossible. Hole sizes vary. They should be as deep as the ice is thick. Never make the hole so wide that you could get a fish through it. Wide holes jinx fishing. Besides, wide holes don't refreeze as fast, and you won't have anything to do to keep you moving if the holes aren't refreezing. And, finally, too big a hole allows the water on top of the ice to drain too fast into the water under the ice and that creates little downward whirlpools.

Now chop a minnow out of the bait pail and breathe on him for a few minutes until he becomes lively again. You are simultaneously breathing on your hand, which feels good, but not for long. Lower the lively minnow down through the ice; if the top water is still pouring through the hole, the minnow will be conveniently sucked down. Attach your line to the tip-up. This is a spring-loaded mechanical device consisting of an anti-suck-through-the-ice base, a spool of line, and a spring-loaded flag. When the fish pulls the line, the flag goes from the down position to the up position. Then everybody runs around yelling "FLAG, FLAG!" Some guy halfway down the lake yells, "Flag!" at us. "Stan," I say, "You gotta flag." It takes approximately nine minutes for all the people ice fishing in Minnesota to start running around their lake yelling "FLAG! FLAG!"

Many times during ice fishing, you won't get a flag. Often, that's because no fish has pulled on the line. Other times, it's a combination of factors. For example, the flag gets frozen into the ice because no fish has pulled on it for such a long time.

I know this isn't an ecology book on Nearctic lake dynamics or a "how to" book on ice fishing, but many

Flagging with dogs

readers will not appreciate the finer points of tippup dogs if they don't understand the niche these dogs are expected to fill.

Oftentimes (once) during the winter when there is no other act in town, Stan will suggest ice fishing. Off we go with the old-fashioned metal tip-ups and ice augers and all the sweaters in the world.

Believe me, it doesn't ever take me more than thirty seconds to remember how miserable ice fishing can be, especially with Stan. Then we get out of the car. Each fisherman on our lake is allowed twelve tip-ups. That means we get to set up twenty-four between us. That means twenty-five holes. (Stan needs an extra for perch jigging.)

We always start off with good intentions, but Stan can't resist testing the waters, so to speak. I've never said this in print before, but (in my opinion) Stan is an obsessive compulsive perch jigger.

A perch jigging rod is normally about a foot long. Stan has a custom-made, three-quarter length, four-piece rod. Each piece is cleverly designed to look like a ball-point pen. You just *know* that when a guy has a collapsible perch jigging rod hidden in his ice outfit, he's not really focused on the job at hand. I've told the therapist about Stan's jigging rod. You never really see it until out it comes.

And it never comes out until the first hole is chopped. "Let's see if there is anybody down there," he'll say.

"Well, you take a look-see," I'll say cheerfully, trying to be supportive and not to aggravate his condition. All the time I'm thinking, *I'm never, never going ice fishing again. Never!* I'll set up the twenty-four tip-ups, after I've chopped twenty-four holes in the ice, I don't mind. And I sort of don't; it kind of takes my mind off how my feet feel.

Anyway, not to make a big deal of the whole thing, I'll drill twenty-four (read twenty-five) holes and carry each of the twenty-four tip-ups to each of twenty-four holes, and set up the twenty-four tip-ups, and hand-warm the twenty-four suckers and reset the flags that have blown loose because the wind is blowing forty-five miles per hour, and if the flag hasn't blown out and over, I'll go look at it to see why not, and it's usually because the hole has refrozen because it's −40°F below zero (−40°C).

By this time, Stan will have discovered half a five-gallon pail full of four-inch perch right in that very first hole. Can you imagine that? If I could just get the Fish and Game people to change the daily limit from no limit to maybe six yellow perch, I'd be a happy truck owner. That might seem a little obscure (and even a little stingy) to a few of you, but realize that it's really cold out there, so Stanley sits in the passenger seat (more leg room) of my pickup (Stanley doesn't own a pickup), with the engine running (better heat), and cleans the eighty-seven four-inch perch on the open glove compartment door.

Tippup Breed Standard and Training

Tippups were developed in Quebec, and I've come across two different versions of how they came about. One tradition has it that eastern Canadian pike pointer fishermen looking for methods of keeping their dogs exercised in the winter were the first to realize that the dogs could stick their heads down a hole just as well as over the side of a boat. I also heard that the tippups were derived from the angler dog whose owners were trying to conserve refrigerator ice and were parking them on lakes in the winter, giving their dogs the best possible face soak. Only an angler dog could enjoy a hole in the ice so much. The other advantage of either breed with their heads in the ice hole is that the hole doesn't freeze up—usually.

But the real story is that tippups were the creation of French Canadians, the finest dog breeders in the world. The rumor is that they ignore all the accepted methods of breed development: if they need a good dog, they simply drive around Quebec until they find a volunteer. The truth of the breed's development lies between these traditions. The original tippup was a cross between the angler dog and the pike pointer.

One time up on Lake Champlain, I was talking to this Vermonter, and one thing led to another the way it does with a Vermonter. He told me about some tippup dogs he was thinking of buying. I'd never heard of tippups. (Technically, that's probably not correct: I had probably heard people talking about them, but it didn't make any impression because I don't speak French. Now of course it is all clear to me when I hear, "Le chien du lac, zat iss un teabeauxp auxp, n'est-ce pas?")

It wasn't long after that until I found myself at chez Jean Jacques Emile Baptiste (Shorty) St. Codeaux at a kennel full of tippup pups. Since he was the third son, he was called Emile. (The fifth son was Shorty.) Emile is one of those savoir-dog guys who knows all the ins and outs of tippupping. The afternoons I spent shouting about dogs with him and his ice fishing buddy, Bugle Bill Stapes, were just pure pleasure. B. B. Stapes always talked LOUDLY because evidently Emile doesn't understand English if it is spoken softly.

In the old days of tippups with straight, skinny tails, when a fish struck and the dog tried to go into tip-up position, the frozen-in tail flag would often prevent the proper behavior, leading to torn flags and nasty back injuries. A kettle of hot water was often a necessity for the first tippup-using fishermen.

Emile's highly bred strain has quilted coat patterns that provide maximum protection from strong winds and precipitation in the hyperzephyrlon. Those with checkerboard coloring are nice—much more sought after than the single-colored ones. The only undesirable color is white: on a big lake during a snow squall, small white dogs get run over by skidooers, which seriously limits their usefulness.

Quilted coated tippups

Emile explained to me that good tippups shouldn't have a lot of feathering on their legs, because they get frozen in the ice. To counter this, Emile's dogs have the fat tail, very much like the fat-tail sheep so common in desert country. But B. B. Stapes told me that the fat tails of the fishing dogs are functionally different from those of sheep. Fat-tail sheep use their tails for water storage.[35] But fat-tail tippup pups grow the tail to sit on. This built-in insulation cushion keeps certain parts of the dog from getting frozen, or frozen in, as it spends vigilant hours looking into its own ice hole. In turn, the heat of the dog's body keeps ice from forming around the tail and freezing it to the ice.

The other advantage of fat tails, Emile explained, is that in the summer he can leave the dogs for weeks without food or water, when his family and B. B.'s go on vacation. The dog can digest its tail fat for calories, and every time it digests one molecule of fat, it gets two molecules of water to go with it, just like the camel. The danger of treating a dog like a camel is that so many dogs are so fat that if people stopped feeding them, they would drown from the inside out.

B. B. described to me the advances in tippup pup ear design. A good working tippup doesn't have either pendulous or prick ears. Both are faults, and it should be obvious why. Let's say your tippup pup had ears like a beagle's and

---

[35] When you digest fat you get water; a camel's hump is actually fat, which stores water. So, really, the way to have enough water in the desert is to eat too much, not drink too much, as is commonly thought.

spent all day sitting motionless in front of its own ice hole with its nose close to the water, watching intently. The tips of its ears might freeze into the lake: think of discovering that just before dark—now what do you do? You could chip out the ice around the ears, making sure you don't chip an ear, take the twelve dogs home, sit them semicircularly in front of the fire, and let the twenty-four clumps of ice melt. But all the way home in the pickup truck, the twenty-four clumps of ear-based ice would have been swinging back and forth at the ends of the pendulous ears, hurting other dogs or denting the sides of the truck.

Similarly, the prick-ear-tipped tippup pup's ears would freeze, making the whole ear like a capless pop bottle top moaning in the wind and driving the dog cuckoo. Cuckooed tippup pups with the wind whistling in their frozen ears make eerie, unpleasant sounds that don't add much joy to an otherwise cold and dismal day.

Tippups with big furry ears that bend in the middle (tulip ears) are now the breed standard. The upper half comes down and inward. A special muscle (the *pinna collecta*) draws the inner side of the upper ear against the inside of the lower ear and across the face of the hole leading to the dog's brain. This prevents the dog from getting frozen ear parts. Some people complain that the dog can't hear when the woolly ear is held tightly in the plug position, but as B. B. Stapes says (and he should know), "They can't hear with their anvils frozen to their stirrups, either." The fur at the ends of their ears is very long and, on really cold days, you should tie them together under the tippup's chin for extra warmth.

Tippups have an *epicanthus* in each eye, giving them a slightly Mongolian look. These *epicanthi* are Lamarckian in that tippup offspring inherit the perpetual squint, preventing snow blindness.

You can't imagine how very excited I became when I discovered these chiens du lac. It wasn't long before I was off to chez moi with a quilted tippup pup and two plastic ice-holes.

Training Your Tippup

It is unbelievably easy to train tippup pups: merely start them young and use plastic ice-holes. Use holes as food dishes; then whenever they want to eat, they will automatically go to an ice hole. Keep slush in the freezer and cover their food with it. This teaches them to keep the holes clean so they won't miss anything. Feed the dogs at random times. This conditions them to look into the holes constantly.

The artificial ice-hole has gone through an evolution of its own. The originals were hand operated and are now something of a collector's item. You occasionally see a reasonably priced one at a tag sale because some widow doesn't know what it is. Early Vermonters used to make them out of leaky bedpans, which were typical of Yankee ingenuity—the bedpans' white color was perfect. The trainer would drop a dog yummy down the pee-wee stem hole at the top, so it would appear suddenly in the larger viewing hole below.

If the stem hole was big enough, I would drop their tennis ball down and play fetch that way. The tennis ball was so much better than a yummy because the dog wouldn't eat what was in the hole, but rather bring it back to you. Some of my very best ice-hole-attentive dogs were trained on bedpans.

Even though tippups became popular, leaky bedpans never did. There was sort of a supply-and-demand crisis for bedpans, with yuppie tippup fishermen resorting to buying new. Vermonters started manufacturing them, and it has turned out to be an entrepreneur's dream. First came the basic model, the dedicated ice-hole, and then a whole series with patented mechanical extras. The self-winding ice hole randomly presents tidbits, mimicking the random pattern of catching Vermont fish. There was an economy model, but it never worked quite right. Some models put out little puffs of dog food odor, similar to a Pavlovian bell, to keep up the dog's hopes that the ice hole will soon yield a yummy. The electric refrigerated ice hole made its own slush.

Nowadays, of course, there are electronic ice holes designed to use the psychological principles of Skinnerian instrumental conditioning. These present the stimulus at irregular intervals, accompanied by appropriate olfactory reinforcers and the slight hint of punishment if the dog doesn't show the ice hole reflex within the prescribed stimulus period.

Really good ice holes come with ozone-friendly refrigeration attachments. The water ices over and prevents the dog yummy from being retrievable. The dog learns not only to keep the apparatus clear of slush, but also to keep his ears out of his ice hole. The tape deck attachment allows you to play arctic sounds, with authentic howling hyperzephyrlonian wind music that is administered with jet nozzles. For about $999.98, you get a pretty nice ice hole.[36]

Personally, I think ice holes have become too commercial. I simply cut a proper size hole in the floor and put in a galvanized bucket filled with water and with half a dozen sinking tennis balls injected with fish juice. The dog will bob for tennis balls all day. When you get to the lake, just throw a couple of the sinking tennis balls in the ice hole and the dog will sit and watch for them. The rest is history.

A friend who has tippups is a joy during holiday seasons. The number of little accessory gifts that can be purchased is practically endless. Monogrammed pads for the pup to sit on are popular items, as are tippup pup pup tents, which are a cheaper (and lighter) substitute for the tippup ice shacks for individual dogs. A little extra money gets you the dog's whole name on it. Tippup harnesses allow the dog to tow his own ice shack to the fishing location. If you are going for the maximum allowable hole number, you could train a team of twelve of them to tow everything out there, including you. The big

---

[36] One severe problem we have at our house is keeping the angler dogs out of the plastic ice holes. Why not buy one for them, you ask? Look, if you think I can afford 1,000 bucks just to make a tongue-soaking dog happy, you're incorrect. The other severe problem is Stanley. When we have him and his wife over socially, Stan always comes through the door assembling his perch jigging rod, ready to jig the dogs' ice holes.

plus is you could race them in sled dog derbies on the weekends. There is no end to the delights of these dogs.

Naming Tippups

I gave Stanley a started tippup pup for Christmas one year, thinking he might take some pride in watching the dog work. But, like so many things, it ended in disaster. Stan goes and names the dog Flag. One Sunday afternoon on Lake Winnipesaukee with the fish biting good, the poor dog ran itself silly. So name your tippup anything except Flag.

Pet Tippups

I don't exactly recommend them as pets. Most of the year, they are okay, but when they shed out, you have trouble. They shed out in the heat of the summer when all the fans are on full bore. It does look funny. Remember those little glass balls with a little house inside and when you shake it, it looks like a house in a snow storm? Well, with a shedding tippup on a hot summer day, it looks like the snow storm is inside the house. The other choice is to let your pet tippup sleep in the freezer, but remember to leave the door ajar. As show dogs, they are wonderful and I love watching judges measure the circumference at the base of their tails.

χ-NOOKY

The thing is, we already have mentioned the χ-nooky without giving away its name. You will remember (if you have read this book from the beginning as you are supposed to) the Home story. Lord Home of late, but not all that late, had mentioned his earlier (meaning really late) relative whose dog was involved in a lawsuit with the Earl of Tankerville because the Home dog was catching salmon and lots of them. Then Our Lord Home had a dog that also caught salmon. I thought about that a lot, because it was suspicious that two Homes had salmon-catching dogs behaving the same way—to me, it was beginning to sound like a breed.

With my investigative hat on, I found that an even earlier explorer Home, a true bastard son of a Home, who—while other explorers were looking for gold, silver, and the Northwest Passage—was looking for the world's best salmon beats. He went all over the world and ended up on the Lewis and Clark expedition to the mouth of the Columbia River looking for the giant Chinook salmon, the veritable Yeti of the salmon world. He and his man/valet/body guard/servant/salmon ghilly (all one guy) stayed on with the Chinook Indians (more on that later).

In this/then primeval wilderness, he discovered a new species of wolf called the salmon wolf by the natives. Being the discoverer of this new species, he named it after himself in Latin: *Canis Chinookii Homesei.* He recognized right off the bat that these wolves had evolved more than your average wolf. They had found an empty niche and were filling it with new techniques of fishing. This evolvedness meant that just about every part of the *C. chinookii* adapts it to catch. The final evolutionary breakthrough was complete when *C. chinookii* began turning salmon fries into wolf puppies.

The oldest (our third story) Home was fascinated watching these wolves swimming, upriver, upstream, upwaterfall, upcreek, looking not just like otters or seals, but more like fur-covered salmon. Their coloration was perfect.

Then it came to him—they were salmon mimics.

They had evolved to look like salmon ready to spawn. Being a countryman of Charles Darwin, he then asked that timely-popular question, "What is the selective advantage of that?"

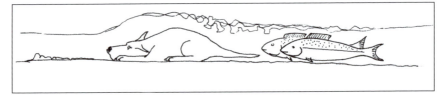

The Chinook wolf—hunting salmon

Home, watching his new species, couldn't believe his eyes when he saw a big buck Chinook try to breed with these stream-lined wolves. These fish would literally swim into the wolf's mouth. Can you believe it? A species of wolf that doesn't do anything—no social behavior—no pack behavior—happy with breeding Chinooks. Home recognized right off that these wolves could be pre-adapted dogs.

Now every Home needs a dog and our Home decided to domesticate his own from these wolves. Once he realized that these wolves would make great dogs, the rest came quickly. Lord Home was a conservative and decided that they should be domesticated the standard way, the way cavemen domesticated dogs. Take wolf pups from the den, grow them up like dogs, and pesto! Tame domesticated dogs! If cave huntermen could get a new breed of hunting dog every fifty years, what on earth were the fishermen waiting for?

Home saw a unique opportunity and went for it. He got his ghylly (archaic, the way an old Home would use it) and told him, "Search ye the wilderness and find ye a wolfie den, take ye some wee puppies, and raise them with ye wee hands and then domesticate them!"

The ghylly blurted out something like, "I don't know how to do that."

But that bastard Home says, "Mesolithic men didn't know how to do it either, but if they could figure it out so can you, if you want to keep the job."

And it came to pass the χ-nooky was born. A dog designed to be sexually attractive to salmon. That was all there was to it. A new breed of dog was born to a British Home with its own backyard and salmon stream.

It has changed the Homes ever since. Now there is no more need for monstrous rods, horse hair lines, boats, nets, flies and streamers, wading boots and hip flasks, when one could have just a little χ-nooky on the side. All he had to do is sit in his garden chair drinking quinine-treated gin while popping delivered-to-hand salmon into the cooler—a true symbiotic relationship.

Well, the Homes were Lords of refined character and dignity. They didn't need to get into the dog-breeding business, so they just kept their χ-nookies to themselves—their own personally derived breed, their own little enjoyable secret for

The χ-nooky—the domesticated salmon dog

generation after generation—occasionally teasing their neighbors with their spectacular results.

But all good things come to an end: χ-nookies never caught on in Britain, partly because so few people are allowed to fish for salmon. And the vast majority of people who don't salmon fish think a Chinook is an attack-trained helicopter. The possibility of radiating from personal wolves into other breeds like all the other domesticated dogs did was beyond imagination and it never happened. Think how the miniature and toy χ-nookies would have made wonderful pets. Aquariums at the dentist's office with a little pack of tiny χ-nookies chasing swordtails. With today's breeding techniques, you could have χ-nookies for every different species of fish. Stanley had one bred up for smallmouths, but he had trouble feeding it.

Eventually a little stray χ-nooky went back to Canada. But the Canadians are a strange people who actually like to fish and don't want any help doing it. Thus, the last of the χ-nookies have gone feral, reverted to the wild, and now only a few wolf biologists know where they are. They have gone extinct as a dog and the only way to get them back is to re-domesticate them.

Training Your χ-nooky

Training a χ-nooky is fairly straightforward. Buy salmon-scented fish oil (available in your better tackle stores) and inject the oil into a tennis ball. Let your χ-nooky puppy chew on the tennis ball. This early period of socialization with tennis balls is very important! When the dog is bigger, you throw the tennis ball and play fetch—which means it brings the scented ball back to you. Then you find a good salmon stream and throw the ball out into the water a couple of times and make sure the χ-nooky puppy brings the ball back to you each time and delivers it to hand. Now just pretend to throw the tennis ball into the water—the rest is history.

χ-nooky names

There is no need to name them because they have gone extinct.

The Sealyhams

The Sealyhams is another great idea in the making. I was faced with a problem of how to teach my grandson to fish. There are several ways to teach a boy to fish and they are all boring.

First: The standard way is go to the local Lake Weedys-cum and fish for sunfish and yellow perch with worms. The only one I knew who actually enjoyed teaching grandchildren that way was Stanley, who would get his perch jigging rod out and finally bore the kid out of his mind. When I asked my local humane society, they said they were against skewering worms on hooks without anesthetics. And they had this poster that claims that children who start out sticking barbed hooks into worms often grow up to be wife beaters or even terrorists.

Second: The only time you can fish Lake Weedyscum is on some unbelievably hot sunny day. Hats, long sleeves, long pants (which I don't think young boys should be allowed to wear anyway. Whatever happened to knickers and long stockings?), and shoes, not sandals. And if the little guy wears sandals, then he has to wear the kind of socks that don't let any light in. And before the kid puts on any of his clothes, you should submerse him in sunblock for about an hour.

Third: Lake Weedyscum is called Weedyscum because it is eutrophic; it has rotting things, like dead weeds, and it has insects. One can buy combinations of sunblock and insect repellent (soaking for a little longer) but neither stop the incessant insects buzzing around, threatening to drink water from your eyelids even if they are inhibited (but not prevented) from biting. Indeed, there are new mutant strains of mosquitoes that are genetically resistant to insect repellent. When the laws about DDT were hatched, I put up a lifetime supply and still have a smudging gun otherwise known as a smogger. They are illegal, but I feel I fall under the grandfathered clause. I'm one of the few great fishermen that don't want that mosquito-fed anemic look all summer.

Fourth: Catching sunfish on a worm teaches nothing about fishing. Why does a smart boy need a grandfather to teach him how to catch sunfish with a worm? There are two good reasons the grandfather is there: first, he is the only one in the family with nothing else to do, and second, somebody has to be there to tell the kid to "sit down!" Besides, I only knew one guy in the whole world that had the patience to clean and skin a hundred sunfish and he (meaning Stanley) did it on my glove compartment door.

"Oops, I got a bite, Grandpa, and here is the fish!"

"Can we take it home and eat it?"

"Will you take it off the hook?"

"Grandpa, it fell off and is gone!"

Tears.

No, no. Fishing is about casting, casting a long cast, hitting the sweet spot, setting the drag properly, giving line, and avoiding breaking a huge fish off. Time, time, time, concentrating, working, thinking, and developing a strategy. It is the sport of fishing. Any damn fool can tell you why they call it fishing and not catching, or hunting and not finding. And you think you are going to teach some seven-year-old to be a real sportsman on a hot buggy day at Lake Weedyscum, catching sunfish on a hook with a worm? Don't be silly.

But none of that for me—I invented the Sealyhams. When my grandson asked if I would teach him how to fish I said,

"Sure. I'd be glad to. Let me get a gin and tonic and I'll meet you on the lawn."

We had a Jack Russell terrier who was hell on rats and mice in the barn. You could teach the dog to chase anything, but it would absolutely not deliver to hand and if it was soft enough he'd eat it right there. This kind of behavior is very rare in dogs except for some of the registered hunting breeds. Once our Jack Russell fetched the thrown object, he would run away and you couldn't catch him. He was the perfect dog for what I wanted. So I got a tennis ball and put a wire leader on it. If you inject the tennis ball with some steak juice, you'll get a better fight out of the dog.

Tennis balls have a nice casting weight to them. A long cast and the dog chases and grab-bites the tennis ball and tries to run with it, and when brought up short, hangs on like a pit bull. Just try to reel him in.

A boy dogfishing

Both the boy and grandpa were happy for days. The boy learned to cast. Bring it back slowly—Wham! The dog takes it

and goes off in a tear. Make sure the drag is right—too loose, too loose, tighten the drag—pop! It broke off. Try again—how do you tie a knot? (Show him how to tie a knot.) Cast it way out—bring it back slowly—a take—Grandpa, I got one on—keep the tip up—up, drag drag, mmm . . . loosen up on the drag—oop! There he goes, slow him—turn his head—no! no! turn his head—Pop, he is off—broke off!

Tie it on again—try a different color tennis ball (kid was fifteen before he learned dogs were color blind)—start again—cast it way out—bring it back slow slowly—doggon! Excuse me, son, this is too exciting, I have to go for another G&T; you keep trying.

You know, I never did ever take that kid fishing. The dogs were so much fun, you didn't need to go fishing. It was catch-and-release, you got a "hook up" every cast and you got an animal so powerful, you could never get it in. And you can do it any time, day or night—weekdays after work—the fishing couldn't be better. Better yet, there were no uncomfortable life jackets, no chance of drowning, no scolding "sit downs," and a new fishing buddy.

Well, I watched and watched and learned. One afternoon, sitting in my lawn chair watching the kid, an idea struck. I bet people would pay to do this. I could have a series of roadside stands that were like miniature golf. You could bring your kids, spend the afternoon. What about girlfriends? That's great. Before the dinner and dance, a little dogfishing. Girls would love it and giggle, and then bend over laughing when the dog breaks off. Then the boyfriend would show her how to tie the tennis ball back on, demonstrating that he was a good provider. He, being knowledgeable, has rented the rabbit-soaked tennis balls. Points! Points! Then she tries again—pop! Oh honey, you got to loosen the drag. "Here let me show you." I always like that one—"here let me show you" followed almost immediately by the "pop," it breaks off, followed by screams of laughter and even hugging sometimes.

Dogfishing is so much better than fishing—so much more action. One can do it anytime with the whole family and friends. You can hear it now, "Hey Hal! Have you ever been dogfishing? No? Well are you in for a surprise!" This could replace team bowling.

There are other aspects to dogfishing, like community service. Aside from educating the whole population of people how to fish without fish and be more self-sufficient, in case of an emergency, think of the benefit to dogs. There are thousands and thousands of dogs out there in animal shelters, put there because they have some bad (sometimes called unacceptable) behaviors, which mostly means that when they chase a ball, they just chew it up and won't bring it back.

These dogs can be rescued. They can bring a purpose to people's lives and bring diverse parts of the society together to have fun and more meaningful play with dogs. And these shelter dogs come in all different sizes, shapes, and colors. It is often said that the dog is the most varied animal in the animal kingdom, even more varied than fish. Think what that means.

What that means is these roadside dog fisheries can specialize—big dogs for men's clubs serving beer and hot dogs—the Fenway frank crowd, and small dogs for little kids and women's clubs serving teas and even rotary lunches.

I have to admit it was a stroke of genius. You don't need a boat—you can rent the tackle—choose the level of dogfishing to match your skills or mood: "I think I'll go light tackle this afternoon." And no waders, hooks, nets, priests (the stick you hit the fish on the head with so you will be more humane) or long car trips to the wilderness burning nonrenewable resources. "Go dogfishing and save wilderness." How about "Prevent forest fires; go dogfishing." "Save endangered salmon; go dogfishing."

Then the second great idea hit so hard, it staggered me. Breed dogfish. Start a project to breed real Sealyhams.

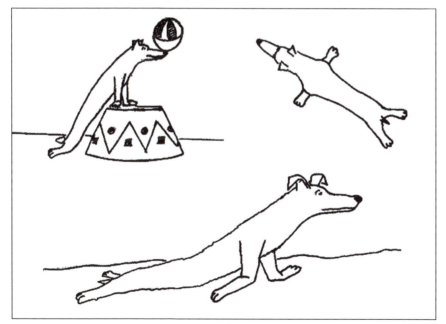

The real Sealyhams

So far we had the χ-nooky that looked like a fish. Instead of having the dog out there on a lawn, you could have them in a tank. You could have the dog in the swimming pool. The χ-nooky swims like a fish. The χ-nooky is a fish mimic. If you can have one breed that mimics fish, you could have more.

Sealyhams (not the real Sealyhams that you all know and love), but I'm talking about real SEALyhams. These dogs are genetically modified to have flippers instead of feet. Everybody knows that vertebrates like dogs originally came from the sea. Flippers evolved into feet. And everybody knows that some of those vertebrates (the whales and seals) gave up feet and went back to flippers and, if they could do it, why can't a dog do it with a little help?

Training Sealyhams

Training Sealyhams is straightforward. You have to start with the right dog. Go to your local humane shelter and take the dogs out one at a time and throw a tennis ball. It doesn't need to have an injection. If the dog chases the ball, you are 50 percent of the way there. If the dog doesn't bring the ball back, you got a winner.

Sealyhams names

I can't believe anyone would need help naming a Sealyham.

Sealyhams as Pets

They are the perfect pet. They are the perfect pet for a kid or a grandfather.

Chapter 11

Making Your Own Dog

I have to agree with the many other experts that the breeding of dogs has gotten way out of hand. Breeding dogs, even good dogs that conform to the standard, always leads to genetic problems—like floppy hips, stiff eyeballs, sticky-out elbows, and weird blood diseases like euphoria.

I have been told by totally reliable sources that purebred dogs are in such bad shape that the English have banned picture-taking at Crufts. At national dog shows, they have these PG-13 signs posted. The British hired a knight and some vassals (landlocked ghillies) to do an investigation. I wouldn't be surprised if they banned dog breeding altogether. The handwriting is on the wall.

Digression: What Is the Problem?

Remember, we talked about it. Breeders of dogs have breed standards and all the dogs within a breed should look exactly alike. If they don't come up to the standard, they are said to have faults. A dog that conformed to the standard would be beautiful regardless of what it looked like.

But therein lies the problem. If beautiful is genetic, and if all the dogs were beautiful, then they would all have the same genes. And if they all had the same genes, then there would be no sense in breeding them anymore because you couldn't get anything else than what you already have. It is simple logic.

Look at it this way. If a breed had lots of different genes, then very few could have just the right combination to look like the standard and most would be said to have faulty genes. But if all dogs looked like the standard, then there would only be one set of genes and that turns out to be the biggest fault. If all dogs were perfect, there would just not be enough genes for the dogs to be healthy or enough genes to keep the breeders busy, and the breed would collapse.

Thus there cannot be a perfect dog—which has been obvious to many of us for years.

So what is next, if there is going to be no more breeding of dogs? If you want an Irish setter, for example, how are you going to get one if the breeders can't breed them? It is a problem!

I was in Holland recently studying this problem. While there, I noticed little Dutch kids are really pretty and they all have the standard national head shape. It was almost like a breed. Little Dutch boys all have the classic Dutch-boy shaped heads. How did that happen? *It must be genetic,* I thought. It seemed reasonable that they had some rule that only Dutch people with the correct head shape were allowed to breed. But then, the Dutch would have the same perfection problems, that the dog breeders have.

But it doesn't happen by breeding. The Dutch have rediscovered head molding. They mold their kid's head to the correct shape. (I know many of you think I lay around in bed at night making up this stuff. Just look it up.) It shouldn't be a great surprise that the mold system works. We routinely mold our kids' teeth into perfect sets. I hardly know any kids between the ages of six and twelve who don't wear braces. In America, all kids go into the required tooth molds and come out with teeth that come up to the American tooth standards. All you have to do is take any kid to a special dentist and, for a couple thousand bucks, he'll build a wire mold that will change the shape of the jaw bone and your kid's teeth will "have" to grow perfect. You don't even have to be young—I have friends in their sixties who are still trying to come up to the national tooth standard after all these years. And (here is the kicker) with no loss of genes. We could all have teeth that come up to standard and still maintain the standard assortment of genes. The clever Dutch figured if you could do that with kids' teeth—then why not do it with their heads?

Why shouldn't we also do it with dog teeth? It ought to be a law that all English bulldogs should wear braces as puppies. And if you can shape kids' heads with a helmet, why on Earth can't you shape dog heads with helmets?

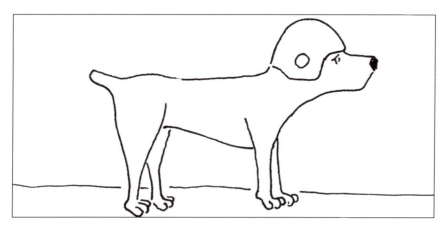

Dutch head mold for dogs

I started with the Baltimore duck heads. Here is a dog that is successful because its head is shaped like a duck. Well, that was tricky breeding. And once you got a dog that bred true, you're in the same old genetic problem. The breeders would get the dogs, write a standard, and then breed the genes right out of them. You'd have a show ring full of ducky heads and somebody passing laws against photographing them.

That was when I hit upon the award-winning idea. Take any puppy dog and grow it up in a head mold that was shaped like a duck. Darned if it didn't work.

Then I went the next step and had specialized molds made by decoy manufacturers. Molds that were pin-tail mimics, teal, eider ducks, you name it and I thought of it.

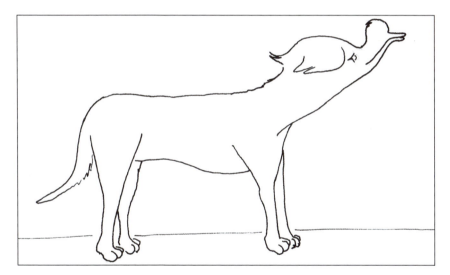

A molded duckhead dog

I got some giant breeds and shaped their heads like Canada geese. I turned a great Pyrenees into a swan. There was no end to it.

The system was very rewarding in many ways. First of all, there are none of those messy genetics like inbreeding or line breeding or back-crossing or back-scratching. Just pick up pups at the humane society shelter and pop them into a mold. There are no genetic diseases involved in creating a breed standard. Here, you can maintain a large genetic variation without worrying about evolution happening. Every dog not only has a perfect head, but also a perfect duck decoy head of the species you want to hunt.

The system has another advantage. Once you develop a good duck dog head, someone wants to buy it. They think it is genetic. I had people that came around and I knew they weren't even duck hunters. *Why*, I'd ask myself, *why would someone who wasn't a duck hunter want a Baltimore bufflehead duck dog?* And of course it is obvious! They thought they could start breeding and selling puppy Baltimore bufflehead duck heads for big bucks. Well, I have to admit, I sold them breeding pairs. Surprise!

I didn't have to tell my secret—besides, molds aren't a secret. You can mail order a head mold out of Holland if you want your dog to look like a Dutch boy. Imagine it, a dog with a human head. I've heard that Hungarians did this and got a dog that not only looked like a Dutch boy, but could also think like one. After all, if you shape the outside of the head like a boy, then the brain has to go in the same direction, I think. The way things were working out for me was I could get three, four, five species of ducks out of one litter of dogs.

Stan wanted to make his own dog right away. Stanley has this stringer spaniel crossed with a tippup just for ice fishing perch. Remember, Stan is an obsessive-compulsive perch jigger. So he'll sit at some ice hole with his stringer × tippup spaniel loyally sitting on his fat tail beside him, letting Stan stuff itty bitty perch into the dog's Velcro quilt coat. The concept of catching a mess of perch took on a whole new meaning.

Stan liked the idea of the Dutch helmets, but he likes to go back to original sources and did this study on the flathead Indians—who turn out not to have flat heads, but the Indians downstream, the Chinook, did. (See, it's all beginning to come together.)

Tiny Digression: Chinook Flatheads— or χ-nook

The aristocratic Chinook Indians put their kids' heads in a press for about the first year so their kids would grow up with flat heads. The reason for this was so they could tell the rich kids from the common kids whenever and wherever the kids were together. If they were watching a hockey game, for example, the common kids would all have helmets on and you couldn't tell who they were, but they could not get helmets to fit the flatheads so you could always see exactly who they were.

Stanley studied the Chinook head-pressing apparatus carefully and made an adaptation for his dog and, sure enough, in a year he had a flathead dog.

This dog had a flat head! I could not believe it when I first saw it. "Stanley," I said, "why on Earth do you want a dog with a head that is flat as a board?" Well, he looked a little embarrassed and explained it was a fillet board for cleaning perch.

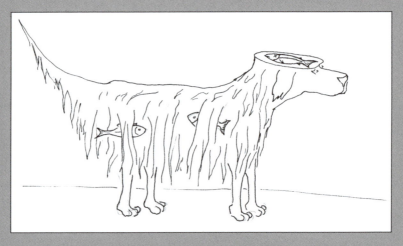

Fillet headed stringer spaniel

He'd call the dog all stuffed with perch and have him sit. Then Stan would just clean fish on the dog's head and at the same time the dog would eat all the scraps. Then Stan would throw a tennis ball in the water and the dog would fetch and come out with a clean head. It was brilliant.

But people were demanding more than some dog with a specialized head. For example, somebody wants a red setter—make a red setter head mold. But there is a lot more to red setter than just the head (most of it bad). That led to the next breakthrough—full body cast. Come on, all through history people have been exaggerating different parts of their bodies. When the Chinese first began manufacturing shoes, they had only invented one size. So they developed these foot molds for baby girls so they would come out with the standard foot size. One size shoe fits all. And obviously there was no loss of genetics there. And peoples around the world stretched necks way, way out like the giraffe-necked women of Thailand. Some thought it made women beautiful, but it was really functional. Stretching necks is the same cooling principle that we discussed in evapo-drooling. No loss of genetics there. Half the people in the world save genes by shaping and painting noses, lips, earlobes, and God knows what else. So if people could do that then *why can't we do it with dogs?*

It turned out to be easy. Making and baking full body molds turned out to be a piece of cake. Take a dog you like and make a papier-mâché cast. You could do it with bronze if you want the mold to last. Bronze molds are very practical for puppy mills that want to use the mold over and over. Most of the time, I used fiberglass and the same techniques you use when making a canoe. From an original positive you could make any number of negatives. For dogs, you just make a mold like if you were laying up a fiberglass canoe. Make a bunch of replicates so you can grow several dogs at the same time.

So how do you get the original shape? It pays to have a good friend who runs an active veterinary service. Making molds from a dead dog is as good as any.

So do I need to say more—make any dog you want—everybody with their very own perfect dog. There will be problems. It will probably put dog shows out of business because every dog in a breed will look exactly alike, which ironically is what kept them in business all these years. I suppose dog shows could change from looking at the conformation to doing DNA testing to see which dog had the most genes. We have 340 dog breeds now, but people can now make new breeds without any of that deleterious breeding—let your imaginations run—we could have thousands of breeds. Dog shows could be like flower shows where people could display new varieties. We could have as many perfect dogs as there are dogs—and *never* lose a single gene.

Chapter 12

Testing for the Perfect Dog

In the transition period between breeding dogs and making your own, there could be some cooperation between the two camps. Think on it—there will be all these perfect dog molds, which most of the time are not being used. So what do you do with the mold? Rent it out to dog testing agencies.

Let's say you got a dog from an old-fashioned breeder, the kind that mates two dogs together to produce a standard but perfect dog. You might think he's a good breeder, but what if he was lying or even just made an honest mistake and bred the wrong dogs together? Thus, you don't know if you got a perfect dog unless you test it. There you are and you just paid big bucks for a purebred red setter. And now you wonder if it really is a pure breed—or is it a good pure breed? (Of course, if it is a red setter, you should already know the answer to that question.) The answer is: you can test your dog to see if it fits the mold.

Digression: Behavior Molding

There are tests that you can give your adult purebred pet to find out if they have the breed-typical behavior. You can test its behavior against some standard which is usually written or is easiest to find out by consulting your nearest behavior therapist. (I have never found one of those behavior therapists who would look you straight in the eye and say "You have a normal dog." Instead, they always claim that my dog needs some professional help!) (And I have never met one of those behavioral therapists that was wrong.)

Not being an expert myself, I consulted with Ken McCort from Doylestown, Ohio, an international expert on behavior modification, who says:

Behavior is the easiest to test. A good pure-bred pet should not have any behaviors that you haven't taught it. Behaviors like barking or growling, jumping up on people, a hypertrophied tail wagging and even door scratching are definitely faults and should have been selected out of your breed of dog. If those behaviors are present, then your dog is definitely not a pure breed. These behavioral faults are definitely too frustrating for the average pet owner to deal with and pets that even hint at any of these behaviors should fall under a money-back guarantee provided by any reputable purebred dog breeder.

For the most part, a perfect pet dog should be seen but not heard, and the most highly bred pets should not move at all unless spoken to. Vocal commands such as sit and stay should have become innate or instinctual for the well-bred pet. "Down" should just be present in the dog ethogram [Ken uses technical terms], and the "long down" with attention to modern behavioral genetics should have become epic in proportion if you are buying a quality purebred dog. The long down should be performed from a sphinx-erect position with a catatonic, glazed stare into space, and the well-bred dog should be able to do this for as long as the pet owner requires, with no real training necessary. Genetics does it all.

Modern scientifically designed dog food should produce no waste products from the dog after consuming it. And finally, dogs bred with low carbon footprints can recycle their own water thus there is no need to housebreak your new dog as there is no need for the dog to eliminate anything it cannot use.

Now if your dog does have behavioral faults and you still love it, not to worry because even though we professionals can't fix it (after all, it's genetic) we can teach you how to live with it.

I don't think I have left out any behavioral discussion, but if you think of something write me.

—Yours truly, Ken

(Ken should meet Barnaby and Craig.)

Always remember that among professionals, shape is more important than behavior. How does the dog look? How embarrassing—there you are at the dog park and somebody says, "What kind of dog is that?" Or they say, "What a cute dog; is it a rescue dog from the shelter?" The worst, "What kinds of parents did the humane society say make up your dog?" "Were there more than two?" How about, "That is a pretty dog; you should have him genetically tested to see what it is."

As the purebred dog owner, you want to see if your dog fits the mold. Molds can be purchased from kennel clubs. Since your mold will probably only be used once, you could think about "rent-a-mold" companies that are sanctioned by the official kennel club. (This brings up an interesting possibility because if your dog doesn't fit one club's mold, you can check it in a different club's mold. This might be a way for an amateur to find the real, official club.)

When your dog has reached the adult pre-fat stage of its development, place it in the mold and close it. If there is screaming, scratching, or bumping around, then you know your dog isn't the right shape and is definitely not of a pure breed (see "money-back-guarantee" above).

If that happens, there are several avenues you can follow. The most difficult is trying to get your money back. The breeder will tell you it is your fault, usually pointing out that you didn't feed the growing puppy properly and that you didn't exercise the dog adequately, both of which will affect the kind of mold that your dog should fit. There is some bone of contention here because breeders displaying their dogs at dog shows would have you believe that their award-winning shapes are genetic and have nothing to do with environmental inputs. But it is hard to explain illogic to a breeder; after all, they are purebred dog experts.

Epilogue

The Tail Wags the Dog

Once you become an expert on something like dogs and especially fishing dogs, your phone rings constantly and hundreds of emails pour in daily. I get lots of emails and telephone calls. Typically, people ask me if I have any good stock tips or tell me that I should vote for the Tea Party candidate or ask how about bomb sniffing dogs. Most people think that since I know so much about dogs, I probably know something else. Often, they use the opportunity to tell me a pretty fishy story about how smart their dog Ralph is.

Sometimes it is a legitimate question about some special health issue of one of their favorite fishing dogs. "Lookit," I say, "I'll see what I've got on conjunctivitis of flounderhounders and call you right back." Sometimes I have to call them right back after a couple of hours to seek clarification. "Is that the left or right eye?" I ask. You see, one eye is in the ancestral position, while the other is in the descendent position, which is moving up. The dog could be suffering from migrating headaches.

Quite often, the questions are about breeding or cross-breeding, say, two different breeds of dogs together like crossbreeding fishing dogs with other fishing dogs or cross-breeding fishing dogs with some normal breed if you can find one. "Why would you want to do that?" I say. Often the answer is, "I've already done it, well actually, the kid left the door open." Crossbreeding is a favorite topic for the wee hours, because this is one of the subjects people don't want to be seen talking about.

All the best fishing dog breeds started with a single individual, since that was the one that had the original mutation. That is the one that looked like what all the rest to come should look like. After the original evolutionary mutation, there usually has been a steady line of deterioration. This is true of all creatures but especially true of dogs. We must strive to stay as close as possible to that original perfection. You can't cross-breed to gain perfection, because you wouldn't know which perfection you'd get (if any). Simply put, no breed of dog is what it used to be; it is practically impossible to get a breed back to its original state even if the line is pure; and if it gets crossed up, by definition it can never be pure again.

There are behavioral problems with crossbreeding, too: if you crossbreed, what is the mutt supposed to do? Remember, to behave properly, dogs are supposed to do what they look like. How can a dog behave nicely if it looks like a crossbreed? For example, if a Baltimore duck head was crossed with a log dog, it might produce a deadhead. Deadheads are old water-logs floating just beneath the surface whose job it is to dent boat bottoms and bend propellers. Stanley always keeps a sharp eye out for deadheads and so far we have been able to outsmart them. Knock on wood.

Even though we know that mongrels make the best pets, the best dogs with kids, the best circus performers, and so on *ad infinitum,* that is hardly the point. Breeders are not in the game to make good pets or circus dogs. (And there isn't a great market for circus dogs anyway.) Breeders aren't opposed to making dogs that are good for something; it is just that that is not their job. Their job is to preserve a breed's original purity and bring the breed up to a visual standard. Given the nature of dogs, this is very hard and takes intense concentration. Besides, pure breeders, like pure scientists, would lose face with their peers if they attempted something useful. Crossbreeding has to be accidental; out of wedlock, so to speak. If it happens naturally, it's kind of okay.

Many people persistently have another crossbreeding motive in mind, namely, the all-purpose dog. The result of crossing two breeds, they reason, could be a dog that does both jobs: a kind of two-for-one deal.

A floating mat dog crossed with a stringer spaniel seems to be a natural, until you realize the dog can't walk home. You'd feel pretty dumb carrying a dog home with fish stuck to it. Fat-tailed stringers would be sought after for their beaver-like qualities, and a Maine bow dog crossed with a floating mat might look rather fetchingly like hemp on the bow of a tug boat, even though it would be impossible for the dog to fetch anything.

Personally, I'd never cross an angler dog.

Stanley is always on me to crossbreed our dogs. "Why do we need all these different dogs?" he asks. "One fishing dog could do everything. Melt them all down into one good Fidue."

"Stan," I say, "You want to breed up a dog that has a quilted Velcro coat; that you could stick seventy-five white perch onto, anywhere, anytime; that has a fat tail so you don't ever have to feed and water it; that floats around the lake casting shade on piscine denizens, which it points out to you with its earthworm-like tongue before it catches the fish itself; and that, just for kicks, has both eyes on the same side of its flat fillet table head?"

"Exactly," says Stanley.

Paddling into the sunset